Praise for the Patterns of Thinking Method

W9-BHQ-194

"As a school administrator, I have encouraged teachers to look beyond teaching the standards and to give students the tools they will need to be successful in life. As a school, we believe that the ability to problem solve and think critically will be key to the success of our students as they will be expected to compete globally. We trained our whole school in the Patterns of Thinking and have seen students engaged in learning like never before. Students now share their knowledge as well as how they have come to know what they know. They are developing a true wonderment about the unknown. Our staff reports that there are more students sharing their knowledge, transferring knowledge, taking risks, and participating in discussions more deeply. The students are taking ownership of their own learning and developing an understanding of systems. Teachers have also developed a deeper understanding of how to give students opportunities that will give them access to learning the curriculum. Using the Patterns of Thinking Method and ThinkBlocks in the classroom has led students and teachers to understand distinctions, systems, relationships and perspectives. It has given them the tools to think about their thinking and knowledge when given a problem to solve or any test of knowledge. As an administrator, I have seen our staff become excited about learning and teaching. We have a well educated staff that provides solid routines, curriculum and expectations for learning, but the Patterns of Thinking Method was the missing link in our school. We are now able to assess how the students are thinking about their own knowledge and thinking. We are now constructing knowledge together. We are truly a community of learners!"

Chris Dickens, Principal, 2009 School Bell Award Winner

"The Patterns of Thinking has brought to the surface all that we know as educators but couldn't put into words. Through the use of this theory and tools my students will have a better chance to access the curriculum that is being provided. I already knew I needed to get my students involved in their learning . . . be active participants. But it's only until now that I am really seeing results. Because of this I am now better able to understand my students thinking. I feel they will be better prepared for their future academic challenges. These are tools that they can use for a life time."

Lenor A. Cummings, Preschool Special Education Teacher

"The Patterns of Thinking Method transformed my teaching practice. It has impacted everything from planning to implementation to assessment. However, the most critical impact has been on the student-teacher relationship. Not only has it allowed me to see how children are constructing their knowledge, it provides a way for me to acknowledge their thinking. This acknowledgment empowers children to explore more ideas and build new knowledge while allowing the teacher to structure experiences around children's current understanding in order to scaffold to a deeper one. What better gift can we give a child than being seen for who they truly are?"

Megan Callahan, Head Start Teacher

"Using the Patterns of Thinking Method with my students has offered me a window into their heads. As a teacher it has allowed me to identify misconceptions and help them construct deeper understandings of concepts. Students have gained confidence through these patterns as well. I have seen first graders make connections and recognize patterns that had eluded me. It has enhanced the educational experience for all of us in surprising ways. Dr. Cabrera and Dr. Colosi are able to explain complex ideas in ways that are straightforward and fascinating. They are engaging and brilliant.'

Jennifer Orr, Teacher

"The Patterns of Thinking and Thinkblocks are not just a cool tool for teachers to use—it is a new challenge to look at the way we as teachers are teaching and the way our students are learning. We can now be equipped to teach our students in a way that empowers them to think and look deeply into what they learn. If we teach students to use Patterns of Thinking then they can truly solve any problem or manipulate any idea. I sincerely believe that students can be successful and set a new standard for a future generation as they are empowered to create knowledge and thinking. We just have to set the example and lead the way."

Lauren Shernoff, Teacher

"Derek and Laura have developed a fantastic tool for students and teachers to understand and interact with content- vocabulary, concepts, relationships, perspectives. Students of all ages are able to make connections through using the Patterns of Thinking Method. It is an essential tool for 21st century learners. Teachers are able to clarify their thinking in the curriculum development or unit/lesson planning process in much deeper ways. ThinkBlocks are an essential tool for 21st century learners."

Lee Ginenthal, District Staff Developer

Thinking at Every Desk

How Four Simple Thinking Skills Will Transform
Your Teaching, Classroom, School, and District

Derek Cabrera, PhD

Laura Colosi, PhD

Research Institute for Thinking in Education
Ithaca, New York

Research Institute for Thinking in Education
Ithaca, New York
www.ThinkingAtEveryDesk.com

Copyright © 2009 Derek Cabrera and Laura Colosi
Printed in the United States of America

All rights reserved. No part of this book may be reproduced,
stored in a retrieval system, or transmitted in any form or by any
means, electronic, mechanical, photocopying, recording, or oth-
erwise, without the prior written permission of the publisher.

Cataloging in Publication Data available
ISBN 978-0-9794308-3-1

All trademarks are the property of their respective companies.

For my mother, father, and Carter
—D.C.

For Gianna, and Elena
—L.C.

● CONTENTS ●

What to Know and *How* to Know

My Alma Mater

My family dinner table was my alma mater. It's the place I learned to love the pursuit of knowledge. It's the place I learned to think. My mother's only hard and fast rule was that we all had to be at dinner every night. Each night we talked about everything under the sun, from the silly to the serious: what we did at school that day, squabbles with my siblings, current events, politics, science, religion, anything.

We played with our food; in fact, we were encouraged to do so. My father had a strange habit of using anything on the table—food, salt and pepper shakers, forks, knives, napkins, and even the plates—to represent any idea he was explaining in whatever topic we were discussing.

"Dad, what do they mean by Reaganomics?"

"Reaganomics is a portmanteau," he'd say, "a word that fuses President Reagan and economics," squishing two chunks of soft bread together. Then he shaped the new piece of bread into a bowl and held it out for us to see. He continued, "Reaganomics has four key components," dropping a piece of diced chicken into the bread bowl as he listed each one. "Reduction of government spending, regulation, taxation, and inflation." And so it continued.

"Dad, what's regulation mean?"

"Well, if you take this large spoon and this small spoon and scoop rice from the bowl, you'll see that the structure of the spoon—its size—regulates the amount of rice that . . ."

And so it went every night at dinnertime.

These early experiences had great effect on me. First, it became virtually impossible for me to eat at my friends' houses. More importantly, adopting my father's habit gave me an eye, a feel, and a love for ideas that led me to the formal study of how we create them.

It gave me an eye for ideas, because I could actually see ideas on the table. Literally. They were no longer entangled in my head— they were right on the table in front of me. Visible.

It gave me a feel for ideas: I could hold any idea in my hand, manipulate it, move it around, and combine it with others. I could take an idea from my brother, change it, add or subtract from it, and hand it back to him. Ideas were literally and figuratively, tangible.

It gave me a great love of ideas: they were to be played with, constructed, combined, interrelated, explored. The world of ideas became my favorite playground. Knowledge became my muse.

While other kids were building skyscrapers and dinosaurs, I was building ideas.

I became fascinated early on with how we make ideas and how we are able to share them with others—this led to more than fifteen years of formal research into the process of constructing ideas among any and all learners. This process is the crux of education.

My father's habit taught me how to construct and deconstruct knowledge. I learned to distinguish and differentiate ideas, to break ideas into parts or merge them into wholes, to make connections between and among ideas, and to consider things from different points of view. In short, I learned how to think.

In this book, my colleague Laura Colosi and I explain the implications of my research into thinking. You will learn some of what we've learned about how thinking works—and how thinking skills can be taught—as the result of our understanding of how knowledge is structured.

Derek Cabrera

August 2009

● ● **O N E** ● ●

Why Students Need
21st-Century Skills

While knowledge and thinking skills have always been important, globalization makes them more critical now than ever before. Globalization creates more and more links, interconnecting people and places that used to seem separate and unrelated. Problems are no longer contained in their own geographical areas but are linked to and impact other problems across the globe.

I don't know about you, but I didn't use to worry about how chickens are handled in China. I do now. You probably do too because a strain of avian flu similar to the one we see today killed 5 percent of the global population in 1918. That virus is now only seventeen hours away from us by plane. Even though Asia hasn't moved any closer to us, it is more interconnected with us. Its problems are our problems.

Our problems in the U.S. have moved closer to Asia, too.

In 2003, one single cow in Washington state caught Mad Cow Disease. In less than a minute, *just the news* of this poor unsuspecting cow's malady traveled—via the Internet—across oceans and continents to South Korea. As soon as South Korea caught wind of the problem on the Web, it banned all American beef imports, costing the U.S. beef industry $850 million. In this interconnected age, even the tiniest things can wreak global havoc.

I'm sure you have googled. When two Stanford graduate students, Larry Page and Sergey Brin, founded Google in 1997, only a gaggle of geeks were googling. They were searching for geeky things. Ten years later, in November 2007, the number of people googling had exponentially increased to 112 million. What was the number one search term that month? iPhone. A gaggle of geeks googling grew in one decade to 112 million people searching for *what?*—a device that allows them to google anywhere, anytime.

At its core globalization is about adding more links. The world gets more and more interconnected one link at a time. But links are like rabbits—they breed and multiply. Hyperlinks beget more hyperlinks, friendships beget more friendships, customers beget more customers, treaties beget more treaties.

I often tell my students that cause and effect are not neighbors on a timeline. Because the world is so interconnected, this is more true today than ever before. Many things that you wouldn't think are connected, turn out to be interrelated in this new world. Strange things correlate. What's the connection between Montana wheat, Louisiana shrimp, and Saudi oil? In an effort to solve the decrease in crop yields caused by pests, we innovated a solution—pesticides. These pesticides led to leeching of nitrates into soil, which traveled via the thousands of streams and tributaries in the Mississippi River Basin and emptied into the Gulf of Mexico. Here, pesticides, which once were a solution to a problem, would now create an even bigger problem. Nitrates created algae blooms that depleted oxygen levels in the Gulf of Mexico, decimating all life in an area the size of Delaware and Connecticut combined. We now call this area where the Mississippi empties into the gulf, the "dead zone," because a place that once provided some of the best shrimping and crabbing in the world is now barren of all life. . . . Meanwhile, the price of a barrel of oil has increased dramatically because of many factors, including the war in Iraq, and many shrimp boat captains can't afford the fuel to get out to the area where the crabs and shrimp still inhabit the waters. Those still in business, naturally, incorporate the price of the fuel into the price of their catch, and your shrimp cocktail just got more expensive. The more things are interconnected, the more often we see the unintended consequences that turn ingenious solutions into deleterious problems.

These ever-multiplying links make the whole world increasingly interconnected, and as a result, problems are becoming intractable, durable, hearty, complex, and tougher to solve. There was a time when "loners in labs" could solve these problems; but modern problems require more knowledge and expertise that any single person can gain in a lifetime. The solutions we need in the 21st century require interdisciplinary "teams at tables." The intractable problems we face—global warming, world health crises, terrorism, even globalization itself—pay no attention to disciplinary boundaries; they cut across social, political, scientific, theological, and financial domains. This will only be more true as we move further into the 21st century. We can't even begin to guess what the coming problems of this century will be. To meet the challenges ahead, problem solvers in this new age will need integrative proficiency in:

- **Content knowledge** They need to know something about an area or field of study.
- **Critical thinking** They need to be analytical and logical in framing problems.
- **Creative thinking** They'll need to think differently to address these tough, interconnected problems.
- **Interdisciplinary thinking** Problems don't respect disciplinary boundaries, neither will the needed solutions.
- **Scientific thinking** They must have a capacity to question, analyze, and use information to address problems in a formal way.
- **Systems thinking** They must understand the interconnectedness of systems, concentric circles of context, and unintended consequences.
- **Prosocial thinking** (emotional intelligence) Because they're working with a team at a table, they'll need to be able to talk, listen and collaborate with others to resolve problems.

We are currently preparing students for jobs that don't yet exist, using technologies that haven't yet been invented, in order to solve problems in a society we can only imagine.[1] The educational implications of this are massive and time-sensitive. As an educator, it is your job to train the problem solvers of the future. It is your job to stock these "teams at tables" with graduates that possess

21st-century skills so that they can solve the world's most pressing problems and contribute to society. Teaching 21st-century skills means teaching students not only *what* to know (content knowledge), but also *how* to know (thinking skills).

Two Laws of Knowledge

In 1900, 8 out 10 jobs involved work with one's hands. In 2000, the statistic flipped—8 out of 10 jobs involved working with ideas.[2] Where schools once needed students to master the laws of the physical world to navigate an industrial age, today we live in the knowledge age. So what do we need to understand today? This is not a trick question. The answer is: the laws of knowledge.

Like the laws of physics, the laws of knowledge are few. They are also simple. But be warned, just like Newton's Laws, what seems simple on its surface can be sublime. Do not let their simplicity disguise the universally important implications of the two laws of knowledge on teaching, learning, and education as well as many other arenas. The epitome of genius, Einstein, once remarked about one of the laws of knowledge, "It was so simple only a genius could have seen it." Einstein knew that the seemingly simple ideas were often the most important ones. In a similar vein, George Bernard Shaw once said, "A man of genius is not a man who sees more than other men do. On the contrary, it is very often found that he is absent minded and observes much less than other people. . . . but, the man of genius understands the importance of the few things he sees." We hope that as you read about the two laws of knowledge in the next few pages you will keep an eye on your own thinking. If you find yourself thinking, "that's not so profound . . .", stop reading and take a moment to think more deeply about the implications of these two simple ideas on every aspect of your teaching and your life.

Both laws have deep roots in scientific research, a long history in scholarly discourse, and complex names in academic terminology. They're brief, instantly comprehensible, and they hold the potential to transform how educators work. Here we go.

We Build Knowledge

The first law of knowledge is—we build it. That's right, we build knowledge. Doesn't seem like much, does it? Let's illustrate its importance with a thought experiment.

Imagine that all of your students show up one day wearing white tee shirts with large black letters that read: **Awaiting Instruction.**

Ask yourself, how will you approach these students? What will you do to prepare to teach them today?

Now the next day all of your students are wearing shirts that read: **Under Construction.**

Ask yourself, how will you approach these students? What will you do to prepare to teach them today?

We've presented these scenarios to educators and other professionals across the country. *Awaiting instructions* conjures up a classroom, with a teacher stationed at the front of the room, the "sage on the stage," presenting a lesson through talk and demonstration. The students act as sponges, absorbing the information as the teacher pours it out. In contrast, *under construction*, conjures up a classroom full of students who are actively engaged in lessons, perhaps through hands-on stations or small-group work, led by a "guide on the side" teacher whose questions are open-ended, and who questions the students frequently. The students in this room are actively constructing their own answers to the teacher's questions.

The crucial point of this exercise illustrates how sublime the first law of knowledge is: regardless of whether the teacher acts as "sage on the stage" or "guide on the side", *students are constructing their knowledge in BOTH situations.* All students are constructivist. The human brain is constructivist. This fact does not change based on classroom setting or teacher practice. Students never simply absorb what is being instructed. Scholars and educators once commonly accepted that knowledge could be moved from one person (a teacher or expert) to another (a student or novice), as files can be transferred from one computer to another. This is simply not true. What actually happens is your students interpret everything they hear, see, or touch in relation to their prior knowledge and experiences, and transform what they're taught into new knowledge through the process of thinking.

Our practice is always a good indication of what we believe. Thus, based on what occurs in our schools you would have to conclude that: 1) it's easy to put knowledge into kids and 2) the relationship between knowledge and thinking is tenuous at best. Yet, the truth is that kids cannot "get" knowledge, they have to build it. And, the relationship between knowledge and thinking is not tenuous, it's nonnegotiable.

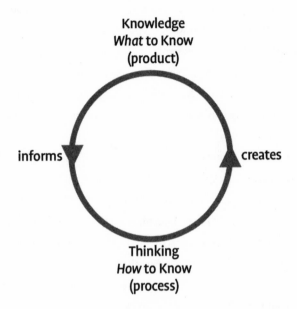

Knowledge
What to Know
(product)

informs

creates

Thinking
How to Know
(process)

Knowledge and thinking exist in an endless cycle. They coexist as a feedback loop in which the process of thinking creates the product of knowledge. This knowledge informs further thinking, which creates new knowledge. Our teaching methods still haven't caught up to this fact. When we think, we build knowledge. When we use someone else's hard-won knowledge we do not receive it as knowledge; it comes to us as information. We then use thinking to process that information into actionable knowledge. We, and when I say we, I mean every living human, do not *get* knowledge, we *build* it.

Knowledge Changes

Equally simple and sublime is the second law of knowledge: Knowledge changes. So what? Seems a bit obvious, no? Yet again, our practice belies our beliefs and desires that knowledge remain static and reliable. We teach facts like they're diamonds, forever. In truth, knowledge is constantly changing. There are three important ways in which knowledge changes: growth, validity, and relevancy.

Growth

The quantity of knowledge grows and expands simply because of the first law: everyone is constantly building it. In the realm of scientific knowledge, we've gone from a handful of disciplines (e.g., physics, chemistry, psychology) to more than 20,000 disciplines and subfields at last count (e.g., biochemistry, genomics, ichthyology, enology). Today there are 338 different "ologies" or areas of scientific study. There are more than 300,000 scientific journals and periodicals. We're inundated with knowledge. For example, it's estimated that there are 540,000 words in the English language today. This is five times more than the number of words that existed during Shakespeare's lifetime. Thus, bodies of knowledge are constantly growing, because knowledge is under construction all the time.

Validity

Facts are neither timeless nor static. Humans learn new things all the time, and as new knowledge comes in, the validity of previously established facts changes. Pluto was a planet. The Earth was flat. African Americans were genetically inferior to whites. Animals didn't use tools, and on and on.

One fact that will never change is that octopi have eight legs. That's because the word octopus literally means "eight-footed." So it's a no-brainer that they have eight legs, right? Right? Wrong. Researchers studying Mavis, a giant Pacific octopus, and Olga, a common octopus, were surprised to find that their most basic assumptions were wrong. In data collected from more than two thousand observations, Mavis and Olga played with a variety of toys, including a Rubik's Cube. Unanticipated results showed that—to everyone's surprise—octopi use six of their eight appendages more like arms; and the remaining two function like legs![3] The facts change over time. Legs become arms, planets become dwarfs, there's even debate about what caused the mass distinction of the dinosaurs . . . stay tuned.

Relevancy

Kids have a knack for finding that one thing that's sure to drive adults nuts. When I was a teenager, it was skateboarding. (Today it might be video gaming.) Avid skateboarders attacked this emerging area of knowledge with all the vim and vigor of new scientists: distinguishing between different tricks, developing new methods of skating—such as pool, ramp, freestyle, and street—and even researching new materials that could be used for softer wheels, better decks and trucks, and skate clothing and shoes. They took to empty pools (and to emptying pools!) so they could develop new "rad" tricks. They turned parks and sidewalks into makeshift skate parks. They raided building sites for scraps of lumber and sheets of plywood to build half and even full pipe ramps. The school's wood shop class became popular because skateboarders needed the woodworking skills to make custom decks and ramps.

In response to all of this, adults—teachers, school administrators, city planners, parents, mayors, and the police—vehemently objected. As skateboarding grew in popularity, so did the official response in the form of prohibition. New no-skateboarding policies sprung up in schools, and no-skating ordinances were posted in city parks and downtown areas. Boards were confiscated, making the wood shop all the more popular.

The overarching reason adults gave for the crackdown was that skateboarding was irrelevant. You should be studying something more useful. Skateboarding, we were told, would not amount to anything. It was irrelevant knowledge.

Of course, it did amount to something. At the 1999 X Games, with more than 275,000 people in attendance, a young skater named Tony Hawk executed the first 900—a 900-degree spin considered to be one of skateboarding's most difficult and elusive tricks. Today, Tony Hawk has his very own skater doll, which can be purchased at any number of stores, alongside his line of video games on PlayStation and Xbox. The skateboarding craze and the extreme alternative sports industry it helped to spawn have not merely provided an arena for a few talented athletes. They have spawned a mega-industry producing anything from cars and clothing to food and beverages, not to mention opportunities for iconoclastic commentary, stage setup, and countless other jobs.

The skeptics were wrong when they predicted skateboarding knowledge would be irrelevant. Those who are passionate and know something about skateboarding no longer seem so misguided. Knowledge changes in relevancy.

Restoring the Balance: What to Know and How to Know

We build knowledge. Knowledge changes. These two laws apply to all knowledge—every subject area, every fact, every idea that ever was and ever will be. They also create an interesting dilemma for our teachers. If what we teach today may change over time, even become invalid or irrelevant, what will our students do as they enter the real world? What will people need to survive in a world where many of the facts they've learned don't survive and the only way to "get" new knowledge is to think? The answer is simple. We must equip our students to approach any new knowledge by teaching them not only what to know (content knowledge) but also how to know (thinking skills).

Content knowledge and thinking skills must be taught in

balance. Yet again, when we look at our schools, we see a dangerous imbalance. We see a mismatch between our practices and reality.

- ➲ We see a system that behaves as if students can "get" knowledge and teachers can "give" it. However, we know that knowledge is built.

- ➲ We see a system that behaves as if facts are static and reliable forever. However, we know that knowledge is constantly changing.

- ➲ We see a system that behaves as if knowledge can be segregated from thinking. However we know that the two are in an inseparable and dynamic cycle.

In sum, our schools are using an industrial age mindset to train students for the knowledge age. If we continue on this path, *every* American child will be left behind. Perhaps most importantly in today's information age, thinking skills are viewed as crucial for educated persons to cope with a rapidly changing world. Many educators believe that specific knowledge will not be as important to tomorrow's workers and citizens as the ability to learn and make sense of new information.[4]

We need citizens who not only know things but can also think—that is, people who can create new knowledge to solve novel problems. Yet, by both commission (overemphasizing content-based curriculum) and by omission (failing to teach them thinking skills) we're letting our students down. Our current situation is a call to action for educators. We must not only teach them what to know but also how to think so that they can create new knowledge when the knowledge they have isn't working. We must develop both content knowledge and robust thinking skills in every student. Instead, we focus almost entirely on content knowledge, testing, memorization, and recall. We seem to believe that children will learn to think on their own: that if we just keep teaching them more stuff, then they will magically, miraculously, somehow, someway, learn to think along the way. It reminds us of one of our favorite cartoons:[5]

"I THINK YOU SHOULD BE MORE EXPLICIT HERE IN STEP TWO."

We don't need a miracle. We need a method. We need an explicit method for teaching thinking skills that really work, that simplify teaching, and that enable any student from preK to PhD to think.

We Don't Need a Miracle to Teach Thinking Skills, We Need a Method

This book provides an explicit method based on four simple rules that underlie the process of creating knowledge. These four rules are simple, sublime, universal, and accessible. Once you learn these four rules, you will find they can be used at every moment with every student in every subject area or grade. In fact, as you learn more about these simple rules, you will see that their utility transcends the arena of teaching and education and permeates into every aspect of life. Sure, the four simple rules will transform the way you teach and the way your students learn. But, they can also transform the way you live.

It's hard to imagine that something as complex as human knowledge and cognition could be rooted in four simple rules. But it is. Indeed, one of the things scientists have learned in the past 50 years or so is that wildly complex systems are, more often than not, based on very simple underlying rules or laws. Examples are plentiful. The evolution of the vast diversity of species and organisms on the planet are the result of simple DNA combinations and interactions. The complex patterns in a sea shell, a leopard's spots, bird flocks, schooling fish, a busy ant colony, or crowded city sidewalks, and highway traffic patterns are all are based on simple rules. Or, reflect on the times you've met truly gifted scientists, CEOs, or sages who despite their near encyclopedic knowledge and expertise, seem to have reduced their craft to a few essential principles. From social systems to natural and physical systems, the most complex among them are not complicated underneath, but simple. Thinking is no different—it is a complex adaptive system with simple underlying rules.

The four simple rules of thinking are foundational to each and every thought that you, your children, your students, your employees, and your loved ones have. What is even more remarkable than the fact that they exist is the transformative effect that these rules have—not only on our students but also ourselves—when we recognize them and explicitly use them in our teaching.

The rules will help you and your students develop their metacognition, or thinking about their thinking. They will provide students with a universal scaffold upon which they build all of their knowledge, access their prior knowledge, and construct new meaning of content throughout their educational experience. Of greater implication is that this holds true for every student regardless of ability, socioeconomic background, language, special needs, or age. The four simple rules apply to every grade, every lesson, every subject, and every student.

From the students' earliest days of watching Sesame Street to the moment when they walk across a university stage to receive their doctorates, these four simple rules will equip your students with all they need to move up in grade level, think through any problem, understand each subject, and prepare them for a certain future in an uncertain, fast-paced, ever-changing world. When our graduates are armed with a powerful method of thinking, known as the Patterns of Thinking, they will know how to do what today's graduates cannot; they will know how to think through anything, especially the unstructured tasks they will face in whatever vocation they choose.

The Patterns of Thinking Method
Making Distinctions

A distinction, of course, implies two things, and that one of them possesses an attribute which is not found in the other.

—Georg Wilhelm Friedrich Hegel

To say that distinctions are all around us is a gross understatement. They are so ubiquitous we often don't see them or forget we are making them. Becoming more aware of the distinctions we make will help us to be more creative, more analytical, and more aware. Making distinctions, on its surface, can seem like a mundane or basic exercise. I assure you this is not the case. The distinctions we make, recognize, or more importantly *don't* recognize, have wide-reaching implications in our personal and professional lives in arenas ranging from science to geopolitics. To see the deep importance that distinction-making plays in our lives, we will take you on a journey through several vignettes. Each one is interesting in its own right, but taken together, you will see how pervasive and important distinctions are. You may also be surprised to see how invisible they are and how often your behavior is based on things that are not in your conscious awareness. Let's get started. From the mountains of Italy to the innards of our own families, from pre-linguistic babies to Pentagon consultants, from geopolitical maps to manipulative motives, from the superficial to the salient and from preschool to PhD, and in both simple and sublime ways, distinction making is a purposeful and powerful aspect of human cognition. Indeed, it is universal to every thought we have ever had, are having right now, or will have for the rest of our days.

The Universal Structure of a Distinction is Identity and Other

Anytime we make a distinction, we assign ideas an *identity* and create, in so doing, an invisible *other*. When we say "us," for example, we are establishing us as an identity. But we are also, inadvertently, often unconsciously, implying an invisible other, "them." No matter what we are thinking we are making distinctions and those distinctions follow this universal structure: Distinctions = identity + other.

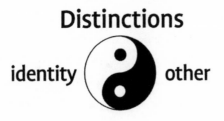

It makes no difference whether the idea is: dog, the Revolutionary War, John's wardrobe, the Treaty of Versailles, Manifest Destiny, Congress, the Town of Ithaca, whatever. Every distinction has the same form and the same rules are followed in order to make it.

When we differentiate ideas, objects, or people, or give concepts a name to discern them from other concepts, we are making distinctions. As we construct an idea of what something *is* we also construct, either implicitly or explicitly, what it *is not*. Creating a distinction draws a boundary—between what something is and what it is not. Indeed, we may often learn a lot about what something is *not* long before we know what it is. In science it is much easier to determine what is not the cause of something than what is. In the lifelong process of learning who you are, you will likely work a lot of jobs or be in several relationships that are clearly "not you" and in the process you will learn more and more about your own identity.

Distinction making is required for the most mundane activity imaginable, as well as for higher-order thinking. There is no pursuit or development of any field of knowledge without distinction making. There is no lecture, activity, or conversation in any subject matter without distinction making.

Read this carefully: a distinction is not a thing that we assign a name to; it is a boundary between that thing and everything that is NOT that thing. The distinction is the boundary that allows us to capture or explicate both an identity and an other. Just as an identity defines other, the other defines identity. Identity and other works much like us and them or here and there. That is, they are relative to each other. Every other is an identity. And every identity is an other. Being more aware of the distinctions you are making (and their underlying structure) will make you more analytically sophisticated, more creative, more systemic in your thinking, and even more emotionally intelligent. Seeing the other when those around you do not will help you to recognize opportunities and pitfalls that others cannot see. Understanding the underlying structure of distinctions will actually make you appear to be smarter.

As we explore a few vignettes about Distinction making, look for this identity-other structure. As your mind becomes more aware of this universal thinking pattern, you will start to see it everywhere and in everything you do. You will start to see how distinctions are made to explain, understand, communicate, and even to manipulate, and you will begin to feel like there's a lot you've been missing.

When We Name Things, It's a Good Indication of Distinction-Making

Because we use language to communicate our ideas, distinction making often means naming things. The way we name things—whether proper names for people, names of files and folders on our desktop, or scientific names—has a big impact on how we see the world.

Finding the right names for things is important. It gives them identity and differentiates them from other things. When the names we give things are vague or too similar, it can lead to confusion, misunderstanding, even chaos.

Heavyweight boxing champ George Foreman named all five of

his sons George. Appearing to be an egomaniac, he claimed this made it easy to remember their names. Over time, it was hard to distinguish among them. George Sr. and his wife ended up giving each George Jr. a number from one to five (literally, George I, George II, etc.). Thus, the name George alone did not allow for a practical distinction among the five junior Georges.

As we develop conceptual models, we often either differentiate too little or not enough. Both are pitfalls of distinction making.

We Don't Need Words to Make Distinctions

When we make distinctions we often think that we need to name them. And although naming can be a good indicator of a distinction, a name is not required. Young children show us that we don't need words to make distinctions. Well before he could speak, my son Carter made clear distinctions on a daily basis. This was obvious at mealtime. We'd give him blueberries, strawberries, and Cheerios and he'd line them up and eat his favorite first. Blueberries, then proceed to strawberries, and then Cheerios. Carter didn't know the words for any of them, but he was clearly distinguishing among them.

Distinction making is a universal cognitive skill that precedes language. While we use language to express the distinctions we make, we don't need language to actually make them.

The Hazards of Ignoring the Other

George Foreman's and Carter's distinction making may seem silly in the grand scheme of things, but make no mistake, the distinctions we make are often serious. In 2004, Thomas Barnett published *The Pentagon's New Map*.[6] The map was a cornerstone of how world leaders conceptualized U.S. foreign policy in relation to terrorism between 2004 and 2009. The leading economic powers of the world ("Us") are called, "the functioning core." The other countries of the world ("Them") are, by implication, part of a not-functional core, or a dysfunctional periphery. (The map labels it "the non-integrated gap.")[7] In this case, the functional core is the *identity*.

It turns out that the countries that made up the "*not*-functioning core" in the 2004 Pentagon map had already organized themselves under the name, the Non-Aligned Movement (NAM) back in 1955. NAM has since become an international organization of 118 states that considered themselves not formally aligned with or against the two major power blocs: the U.S.A. and Western Europe vs. the U.S.S.R. and Eastern Europe. Most member nations had suffered the imperialism of at least one of these at some point in their history. NAM strove from its inception to provide a group identity for its member nations through non-alliance (with the others) and to strengthen themselves through alliance with one another. NAM's 118 states all come together to differentiate themselves through *non*-alignment.[8]

Alienating or ignoring the other can be detrimental. As Sun Tzu said in *The Art of War*, "If you know your enemies and know yourself, you can win a thousand battles without a single loss. If you only know yourself, but not your opponent, you may win or may lose. If you know neither yourself nor your enemy, you will always endanger yourself." Whether you choose to recognize the invisible other in order to empathize with him or to defeat him, the maxim remains the same: as a 21st-century thinker, you must see both the identity and the other in every distinction you make.

We Get Our Identity from Our Relationship with the Other

There's a tribe in Northern Natal in South Africa that uses the greeting *Sawubona*—literally translated, "I see you." Once seen, the person being greeted responds, *Sikhona*, or "I am here." The exchange is born of the spirit of *ubuntu*, a word that stems from the folk saying "A person is a person because of other people."

In other words, our identity is based on recognition by another that we exist. We are all defined by how we relate to others in context. At home, we are "mother" or "wife" to those around us; at work we are "CEO." This is in contrast to our typical notion that our identity comes from within; in fact, we get our identity from those around us (others). Identity and other are two sides of a single coin. *There is no identity without an other.*

Lost Identity

No man is an island, entire of itself.   —John Donne

In September 2006, a man woke up on a street in Denver, Colorado, with no idea of who he was, where he was, or how he'd gotten there. Having no name, no identity, he was checked into a hospital as "Alpha 74."[9] There, medical personnel found no head injury or tumor to explain his amnesia. Officials administered truth serum to make sure he wasn't feigning his forgetfulness. In the end, he proved to be such a good, honest guy, they started calling him Al. Not his name, but a more human version of "Alpha 74."

"I want my past," Al kept saying. He even made an appeal on national television to anyone who might know his identity. He needed an other in relation to whom he could find his identity and be himself. His past, if he could find it, would tell the story of who he was and provide those others who ultimately defined him. Without all of that, he had no identity.

The TV appearances worked. Al was identified as Jeffrey Ingram and returned to his home in Olympia, Washington. Once he found others, he also found his identity.

You Are entering Not-Cadola

It's common in the United States to be greeted with a sign that reads, "Entering Smallville," when driving into a town by that name, and "Leaving Smallville," when driving out. These signs demarcate the distinct area that is Smallville. These signs mark the boundaries of that town. This is in contrast to towns in other countries, for example, Cadola, Italy. We encounter the same type of sign upon entrance, but as we drive out at the other end of town, the same sign shows up again—but

crossed through with a red line. As we leave Cadola, we enter not-Cadola.

Figuring Out What Something IS by What it is NOT

The children's book *The Bus for Us* [10] shows a brother and sister standing at the bus stop on a school day. A classic yellow taxi rolls in. "Is this the bus for us, Gus?" asks the little sister. The big brother answers, "No, Tess. This is a taxi." A big blue vehicle with pulleys and cables comes along next. "Is this the bus for us, Gus?" asks Tess, only to be told it's a tow truck. This exchange continues with a fire engine, an ice-cream truck, a garbage truck, and a backhoe, until finally the big yellow school bus shows up and Gus gets to say, "Yes, Tess. This is the bus for us. Let's go." So Tess learns what a bus is through what it is not.

Of course, that's not the only distinction being made here. There's also that of *us*. A bus could come by that's the bus for *not-us*, or for *them*, and Gus and Tess would need to make that distinction and stay put instead of climbing aboard.

Distinction Making In Seconds or Years

The making of distinctions is so pervasive, so ever-present, that it is hard to recognize all of the distinctions that are happening around us all of the time. In less than a second, we are making dozens or more distinctions. Then, in another split second, those distinctions morph into new ones. Distinctions occur in fractions of a second within our own minds, but they also occur over weeks, months, years, decades, even centuries as social groups and whole cultures struggle to define things. Let's look at three different distinctions—two that happen fast in your mind and one that occurred slowly, over many years, and among many minds.

The way you interpret a Rubin vase (created by Gestalt psychologist Edgar Rubin) depends on how you define the borders of the drawing. Look at the white area of the image, do you see a vase? Now look at the black area, do you see two faces? With a little concentration most people will see both face and vase. But, is that all you see? No matter how many times you ask, people tend only to see the identities: the faces and the vase. But what you are actually seeing is four variables: face and not-face and vase and not-vase. Notice, too, that we can't see both at the same time. When we're looking at the faces, the vase no longer exists as vase but becomes simply not-face. Likewise, when we focus on the vase, the faces become the other, or not-vase. As you can see, an awareness of identity-other allows us to see more possibilities; and therefore, the depth of our understanding expands.

What we choose to see or are able to recognize changes everything: how we think, how we behave, and how we understand the world.[11] Anytime we make a distinction, we decide to recognize some things and to ignore others. We make one thing primary and another secondary.

Let's try another example.

What do you see? Old woman or young lady? Both are in the picture. Again, it's all in how we draw the boundaries. If you see the young lady, take another look at the necklace she is wearing. It is the mouth of the old woman. The Rubin vase and the image above are distinctions that occur in seconds inside your mind. Yet, even in this tiny time span, we can see that our thinking includes elements that are part of our consciousness and other elements that lie beneath our awareness. The first Pattern of Thinking—distinction making—will help you to see more of the processes that you or your students are using to build constructions of the world or to conclude things about it.

Now let's look at a distinction whose boundaries were interpreted and drawn not in seconds by one mind, but by thousands of highly-trained minds over years and years. There's been a sort of galactic patriotism in knowing there are nine planets in our solar system, and they are, in order of increasing distance from the sun, Mercury, Venus, Earth, Mars, Jupiter, Saturn, Uranus, Neptune, and Pluto. In the English-speaking world, we've had a mnemonic device to remember the order and we've taught it zealously to our children and students: My Very Educated Mother Just Served Us Nine Pizzas. Never mind all that; even the most sacred knowledge can change. So now, perhaps our mothers can simply serve us Nothing, as Pluto was recently stripped of its planetary status.

Pluto made headlines when scientists decided it was not actually a planet.[12] While we all learned of this change from planet to *not*-planet in an instant, in fact, changing the distinction took years. It was determined through an official vote at the General Assembly of the International Astronomical Union (IAU) in Prague in 2006. Prior to the vote, of course, a whole process took place. Individuals and teams conducted research; research findings were shared through refereed journals and conversations; people engaged in impassioned debates, and some spoke before the group at the IAU conference. One person alone can create a new distinction in seconds (as we saw with face/vase and old/young woman), but a group takes much longer to gather the evidence and come to an agreement. Yet, the elemental structure and process remains the same: a distinction is made up of an identity and an other.

In 2003 a celestial body was first identified that was situated beyond Pluto in the solar system.[13] (Knowledge changes by growing.) Nicknamed "Xena," this object was determined to be larger than Pluto and, like Pluto, to have its own moon.[14] This put the scientific community in a quandary, forcing a redefinition of the concept of *planet*.[15] As knowledge changes, distinctions once made must be revisited and revised. That's how Pluto became a dwarf planet.

Clear Boundaries Are often Fuzzy

We often imagine that boundaries are more solid and clear cut than they truly are. For example, the border between Italy and Austria is well defined on a map, but in reality, there is no solid line painted across the landscape The distinctions are actually cultural and historical, and they don't clearly fall on either side of a solid line.

If you travel the Alps from Italy to Austria, your trek will take you through the land of the Ladins.[16] The Ladin people, who share this region with others who identify more distinctly as Italian, speak their own language, also called Ladin. It's neither Italian nor Austrian German; it's similar to both and unlike either. In Ladin, you'll find that dumplings and sauerkraut show up on your plate well before you hit the Austrian border. You might feast on pasta and strudel in the same meal. But before you walk into the restaurant, be sure to notice how the architecture blends Italian and Austrian components. The history of this region is a story of shifting distinctions and redefinitions, as the land passed back and forth between Austria and Italy. It even belonged to Tyrol at one point. Anyone remember Tyrol?

The concept of fuzzy boundaries doesn't stop at the geographic or geopolitical level. When you zoom in wherever borders and boundaries exist, even in the conceptual realm, things blur. All distinctions start to get fuzzier, even between or among ideas. This is why such heated debate occurs when experts split hairs—because at that resolution nearly every clear-cut boundary gets fuzzy.

Fuzzy boundaries are everywhere. Even as you sit and read this, there is a distinction between you and your chair—which isn't as clear as you might think. On a molecular level, there's no line drawn between you and the chair: you're a clump of molecules, the chair is a clump of molecules, and molecules are not static. The molecules of the chair form a solid and interact with one another more strongly than they interact with your molecules. (This gives the chair its "chairness" and you your "youness." It also gives you a place to sit.) Still, a little of the force that binds objects together leaks out, and your molecules spend some time mingling with those of the chair. Thus, on a micro level, you're part of the chair when you sit on it, and the chair is part of you.[17] The boundary is fuzzy.

Because Boundaries Are Fuzzy, They Can Be Manipulated

Between 1810 and 1812, the quaintly-named Elbridge Gerry served as governor of Massachusetts. That was plenty of time for his party to produce an electoral map carefully planned to maximize the number of seats it could win. One district was thought to be shaped like a salamander and was famously depicted by a cartoonist of the time. Thus, the word *Gerry-mander* was born.[18]

In modern usage, *gerrymandering* refers to aggressive redistricting in which one party reapportions voting districts so as to increase the number of seats it will hold in the legislature. Because this is done by the party in power, gerrymandering favors incumbents. "Put in simple English," writes P. Harris of the British independent newspaper *The Guardian*, "gerrymandering enables politicians to choose their electors. Not the other way around."[19] Harris also (with some relish, and also with accuracy) describes a map showing American voting districts: "They are far from logical or square. Instead they are wild shapes, huge ink blotches spraying in every direction like some weird Rorschach Test. They are also a fundamental threat to American democracy."

It's important to teach students that the boundaries we draw to make distinctions are not superfluous; they have great purpose, meaning and impact. When we teach our students about distinction making, we inoculate them from an onslaught of manipulative messages (from media and political sources) that are vying for their time, attention, votes, and dollars. When we are made aware of the structure of our own thought we are much less susceptible to manipulation whereas when our thoughts are hidden from our view, we are easily swayed. Hitler said, "What luck for rulers that the people do not think." He was right. Distinction making, like each of the four Patterns of Thinking, can be an implant or an inoculation. It is why thinking in general is patriotic—an essential component of any democracy.

THREE

The Patterns of Thinking Method
Recognizing Relationships

Carl Jung writes, "*The meeting of two personalities is like the contact of two chemical substances; if there is any reaction, both are transformed.*" Jung was making an observation about the deep similarities between two very different subject areas: chemistry and psychology. He saw a common structure in relationships despite the vast chasm between their domains. It is true that when two chemical substances react, both are transformed in the same way that when we meet another person, our lives are altered in some small or significant way. This holds true when we make a relationship between two ideas; the meaning of both constructs is transformed. This is the second pattern of thinking: relationships.

Relating ideas is so universal that we cannot make a single distinction without also making a relationship; a distinction is the relationship between identity and other. In turn, once we have a few ideas distinguished from each other, we can begin to relate them. When we do, like Carl Jung said, both are transformed.

When we relate the ideas A and B, A will have an "A-like" effect on B, and B will have a "B-like" effect on A. But of course this cause and effect relationship depends on what A and B are in the first place. Let's say you are given two ideas, A and B, and asked to relate them. You are told that A is a grade on a test, so you'll naturally think of B as a lesser grade—the meaning of A has caused you to interpret the meaning of B to also be a grade. Alternatively, if you are told that B is a team in a volleyball tournament, then you'll think of A as another team. So, whenever we relate two ideas, each one causes, and in turn, effects, the meaning of other in a reciprocal dance—an interrelationship of cause and effect.

In our workshops, we use a simple and powerful exercise to show the way ideas in a relationship transform one another. We begin by writing the word *coat* and asking a participant to describe it. Usually, participants describe a coat based on the season, so in winter they might say it's warm, brown, and hip-length. Then we present the word *lab* and ask our volunteer to relate the two words and to describe the coat again. Whatever the coat looked like before, it now becomes a long button-up white coat, made of cotton, and with a pocket for pens. Then we add a third word. We put in the word *dog* and ask them to describe the coat again. In an instant, the coat becomes the fur of a Labrador retriever. Of course, what also changed was the person's concept of lab, which initially was a scientist's laboratory and then became a Labrador retriever. This sequence of conceptual transformations elucidates the hidden and universal structure of the second pattern of thinking: Relationships = cause + effect.

Relationships are universal to thinking. We all relate things. We relate to one another. We understand our own identity based on those that we are related to—the people around us. All fields of knowledge are created by establishing relationships between and among ideas, disciplines, or entire areas of study. We make connections, associations, and links all the time; at the foundation of each is the hidden structure of relationships. The following examples range from superfluous to serious, but they illustrate four key points about relationships:

1. they are universal,
2. they are often hidden or implicit,
3. they are distinct and often are systems themselves made up of parts, and
4. relationships are *inter*-relationships between and among ideas.

Discovering Hidden Connections

Nature rarely reveals her secrets, especially when it comes to how things are related. When we look at nature it's often easy to see distinct objects or animals, an individual plant or tree, or an entire ecological system like a pond or a greenhouse. It's easy to see the parts of a bridge or a building or distinguish between snowflake crystals or cloud formations. What's really difficult is seeing that which is invisible—the relationships that exist between and among the visibly different parts. When we teach our students to see relationships as an explicit part of their thinking, we are teaching them to see with their mind's eye what they cannot see with the naked eye.

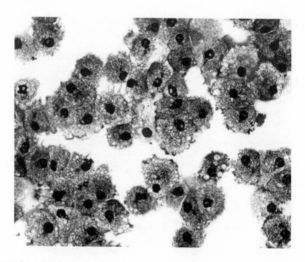

Take a look at the cells in the image above. You can see the cell walls, the nucleus, the plasma, but you cannot see the relationships between and among those parts of the cells. Now imagine you are teleported to an unfamiliar dinner party. You can see individual guests but you cannot see the relationships between them. Would you think differently if you knew they were all employees of the same company? Family members? Teachers? Relationships matter. The relationships between and among things determine the dynamics of the situation or system. The tricky part is that these incredibly important relationships are often totally invisible. To survive and thrive in the world, we must understand the reality of what's going on, but we're not seeing the whole picture. Without making the invisible relationships visible, our understanding of the world, problems, situations, events, organizations, and people is incomplete.

Because relationships are so often invisible, we must have cognitive reminders to help us make them more visible, more explicit. We must ensure that students are making these connections so they can build new knowledge. And when students recognize existing connections, they gain a deeper understanding of what they are studying. The second pattern of thought—relationships—tells us that relationships are universal, and that even when they are hidden, we need to look for them.

To engage students, a teacher must know them for who they are. To know students, a teacher must not only understand the distinctions they are making but also the invisible relationships that influence the meaning they make. Because children are constantly making relationships—often without acknowledging them—teachers must be aware of the influence these relations have on children's thinking and understanding.

It is equally important that the teacher helps the child see the many potential relationships that exist between ideas. But how do we guide students to see them? Here's one simple example that will have dramatic effects. Worksheets that ask students to relate selected items are ubiquitous in schools. Typically, the child is given a worksheet that has several images or words with the assignment to relate the items by drawing a line in between them. When the child draws the line, we know that he has constructed a relationship but we know very little about what that relationship is in the child's mind. To understand the child's constructions, we need only ask two simple questions. Let's take a look. Say the child finds mom and dad on a worksheet and draws a line between them:

Mom ——————— Dad

What does this line tell the teacher? Not much. We know that the child intuits (or has guessed that there is a relationship between Mom and Dad), but we don't know what his construct is for that relationship. By combining distinction making with recognizing the relationship, we can ask the student to name the relationship. This tells us what his concept of the relationship is—because naming the relationship establishes its identity for the teacher and the student. If a student labels the relationship "marriage" or "love" or "me" or "fight a lot" we gain powerful insight into his thinking.

Mom —— *marriage* —— Dad

Once the relationship has an identity (such as marriage) we ask a second question based on systems thinking (you'll read more about this in the third pattern of thinking): What are the parts of marriage? As a student identifies the parts of the relationship, teachers see the child's construct of the idea "marriage." When students relate two ideas, name the relationship, and explore its parts, the teacher can see how students are thinking. If we are what we think, then the teacher is getting a window seat into the child's mind. By prompting the child, will see his own thinking and be more capable of seeing its value or correcting it when necessary.

Interrelationships Lead to Interdisciplinarity

When we relate things, we make new knowledge. Knowledge becomes more interconnected. As students find more relationships among ideas it increases inter-disciplinarity, transfer of learning, analogical thinking, creativity and innovation, and the ability to form new ideas by combining disparate pieces of prior knowledge. This is what we need: graduates who can make relationships explicit in the course of solving difficult problems that we face in this interconnected world. It makes no difference whether students are 5 or 85 years old—prompting them to see invisible relationships (and distinctions) will deepen their content knowledge and make them more sophisticated thinkers at any age and in any topic. In turn, they'll be invited to the table—to be part of the team that solves the world's most pressing problems and makes society a better place.

Here's a real-world example of how seeing a new relationship not only led to new knowledge but to a whole new discipline. Before it was recognized as a discipline, biochemistry began as informal relationships between various types of formally trained people. Chemists, biologists, physiologists, immunologists, physicists, and botanists—all curious about the chemistry of biological processes—began to talk and share information. Over time, as scientists engaged each other, the relationships grew and grew. Scientists began to distinguish biochemistry as a separate but related identity of its own. Today biochemistry is a field of its own. It is no longer just an invisible relationship between biology or chemistry. Biochemistry has its own publishing venues, its world-renowned scholars and experts, its exclusive conferences, and its own accruing body of literature. In short, it has taken on a life of its own. It even has its own perspective, so that someone might approach a problem by asking, "What do the biochemists think of this?"

The birth of biochemistry—from an emerging relationship to a distinct field of knowledge and a complex system of scholars, journals, and conferences—shows us no less than the future of science; which lies in our combining any two (or more) disciplines. Each combination holds new potential because it addresses something that isn't yet addressed by current fields of study. Currently, 20,000 named disciplines of knowledge exist. Out of these, there are 199,990,000 new disciplines we could hypothetically create based on all the possible paired combinations (not to mention threes and fours). We've only begun to harvest the possibilities with the likes of econophysics, astrobiology, evolutionary psychology, information technology, and even bioinformatics (the application of information technology to the field of molecular biology).[20]

Each time a new "hybrid" discipline comes into being, it follows a similar process. First, two fields exist as distinctly different. Someone begins—or, more likely, a few people begin—to relate them. The relationship is implicit at that point. When the relationship grows and begins to have component parts—when it starts to develop into a system—then it is acknowledged as something in itself as opposed to existing as a relation of two other fields. Then it is named and comes into being as a distinction, which encourages further development of its function as a system, and on it grows.

This remarkable process—relationships evolving into a system that solidifies into a distinction with its own perspective—not only births new fields but actually creates permanent changes in our way of perceiving things. It creates true paradigm shifts. We can only begin to imagine the new fields coming in the future and the impact they will have on our research, our technologies, and our lives.

Building New Knowledge

If the value of relating two disciplines to form a new one isn't enough to elucidate the sublime importance of relationships, consider that the very same processes described above are also occurring constantly between individual ideas on a much shorter time span. Creativity and innovation, the creation of new knowledge and new ideas, and the epiphany that leads to the next million dollar invention follow the exact same processes—relationship, distinction, system.

There are three ways to innovate. First, you can invent something totally new. That's not easy to do. Second, you can make an existing thing better. That takes some skill. Third, you can relate two existing things in a new way. That's an algorithm for creativity and innovation that's used again and again by inventors and entrepreneurs. It involves recognizing a relationship between two products or services that no one else has put together before such as minimarts and gas stations or a cell phone and email.

Let's look at the birth of an idea that has changed an entire field of knowledge. Not just any field. Design. The field that is responsible for every piece of technology you and your students use, from your laptop to your cell phone to your car or your hair dryer. The spark for the idea that changed the world was simple: it was born of a relationship. There was a time, not long ago, when designers saw their job as designing a thing—a cell phone or a toaster. Today, the new field of interaction design has changed how designers think about designing. "Designers of digital technology products no longer regard their job as designing a physical object—beautiful or utilitarian—but as designing our interactions with it."[21]

But it wasn't always called interaction design. Bill Moggridge describes his first presentation on the topic at a conference. With the distinction still fuzzy, he called it "'Soft-face,' thinking of a cross between software and user-interface design."[22] Because Cabbage Patch dolls with their mushy faces were ubiquitously popular at the time, a friend of his convinced him to find a name that didn't evoke that image. Thus, the term interaction design came to be. He created it with Bill Verplank, another pioneer in the field who writes, "as there was not yet any education in interaction design. . . . by the end of the eighties, we were starting to feel that we had momentum, and that we could declare ourselves to be interaction designers."[23]

These people who call themselves interaction designers are important to me and you. They're the ones that are going to make it so my mother can use email and you can connect your classroom to classrooms around the world. They're the ones that are going to make us sit more comfortably in our chairs, avoid carpal tunnel in our wrists, or safely drive and chat on the phone at the same time. Their work touches all of our lives everyday. The spark of genius that made it all possible was seeing a relationship between two things that no one had seen before. That little relationship changed Bill Moggridge's life and it's still changing yours and mine.

Implants or Inoculations

When relationships aren't stated explicitly, it often behooves us to bring them to light and name them. Nowhere is this more important than in the way we receive media presentations, whether from news or advertisements or propaganda put out by any organization. Anyone presenting any idea with a motive (whether good or bad or anything in between) is likely to create and put forth relationships between concepts—and these are often left implicit.

We cannot question our thoughts if the relationships we draw remain invisible. Worse, we cannot question what is handed to us by others if we allow the relationships *they* draw to remain invisible. Consider the work that goes into creating implicit relationships in business or politics. A single marketing executive or political operative (or their teams), armed with great understanding of human thought processes, can construct a single campaign designed to manipulate hundreds, thousands, or even millions of people to do, buy, or vote for something. They take a great deal of time to craft invisible relationships to present in a speech, in an ad, on a flier. We often take only seconds to receive what they create.

During those seconds, as thinking individuals, we must look for invisible relationships. We must make those relationships explicit for ourselves. We must teach our children and students to make relationships explicit, too. Our task is to determine what relationship exists (or is being posited) in the ideas we encounter. From there we can ask, "Is it valid?" "Is it true?"

If our own thoughts are not visible, then they're not our own thoughts; they are thoughts given to us by design. An unthinking populace is a dangerous one because the many can be manipulated to the ends of the few. Implying that a relationship exists between two ideas is a powerful tool used to manipulate us for our money, votes, or attention. Relationships are often implicit, and it is crucial that we recognize them. The simple act of recognizing an implicit relationship that has been made *for* us therefore serves as an inoculation against these manipulations. So, this second pattern of thinking—recognizing relationships—is another seemingly simple task that has profound implications for our children, ourselves, and society.

FOUR

The Patterns of Thinking Method
Organizing Systems

The simplest definition of a system is "two related things." So, the first pattern of thinking allows us to distinguish between different things (a car, boat, the French Revolution, Snuffleupagus, Big Bird, homeostasis, mergers, acquisitions, towns, countries, whatever). The second pattern of thinking lets us begin to relate things (e.g., husband-wife, predator-prey, meat and potatoes, Simon and Garfunkel). When we distinguish between and among things we make them different but when we relate them we make them part of a system. Thus, the third pattern of thinking is "Systems."

So many of the things we can say about making distinctions are true for organizing systems, too. To say that distinctions and relationships are all around us is a gross understatement; the same is true of systems. Systems are ubiquitous—they are part of every thought in every moment of every day no matter the situation. If, in a nutshell, distinctions are how we name the world, systems is how we carve it up into parts or lump it together into wholes.

Seeing things as parts and wholes seems like a basic skill, but like distinction-making, it has profound implications on our students. When students see the systemic properties of things, the distinctions they make become more detailed. They see both the coarse- and fine-grain aspects of an idea. They re-draw existing boundaries on systems of knowledge, making them aware of the short-sightedness of fixed categorical thinking. They begin to routinely challenge the categorical groupings made in any field and recognize the very perspective from which the grouping originated. Boundaries that once existed in their minds are removed, as the infinite embeddedness of parts and wholes becomes clear. Students see knowledge as it is—fluid and interconnected. Ideas are no longer static facts that exist in isolation; they are seen nested and connected with other ideas around them.

When students understand that knowledge is structured in parts and wholes relating to one another, they are intuitively given the power to both construct new knowledge or de-construct and better understand existing bodies of knowledge. They gain a cognitive foothold into how to analyze and explicate entire systems of thought. Ideas are more easily explored, connected, and nested among a vast array of other ideas.

The Universal Structure of a System is Part and Whole

When we think of a system, we are thinking of much more than we realize. By implication, we are thinking about the parts of that system and understanding how they relate to form a whole. Thus, the elements of every system are parts and wholes. So we can say that: Systems = part + whole.

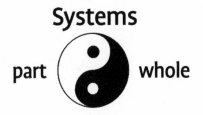

All knowledge has part-whole structure, and therefore to understand it, we must see the part-whole structure of each and every idea we encounter. It is easy to see; the universe at every level of scale is organized into a part-whole structure. We cannot grasp any field of knowledge without seeing the part whole structure of systems. There is no idea in any subject matter that is not made up of parts and wholes.

Read this carefully: a system is not a thing, it is a relationship between or among the parts and the whole. There are many types of systems, from physical to conceptual, from the superficial to the salient. Systems can be wildly different from each other, but one thing they have universally in common is their part-whole structure.

Every whole has parts and all parts are wholes. Seeing part-whole simultaneously is a crucial part of organizing systems. Note, too, that "parts and wholes" works much like "identity and other." That is, they are relative to each other. Every part is a whole. And every whole is a part. Seeing that any idea is both a part and a whole is foundational not only to systems thinking, but to all thinking.

These few vignettes—from Russian nested dolls (matryoshka dolls) to ecological systems, as well as everything between and beyond—show that the part-whole structure underlying all bodies of knowledge can't be missed. As your mind becomes more aware of this universal thinking pattern, you will start to see it everywhere and in everything you do.

Seeing Systems

Laura's daughter Gianna was struggling with math homework and asked for help. "Fractions, ugh!" she said. I told her that fractions might seem like numbers and math but really they show up all over the place whenever we break something down into parts. That's because fractions are merely part-whole thinking disguised as math. Gianna was skeptical. (What self-respecting seven-year-old wouldn't be?)

"Bring me something and I'll show you," I suggested.

"Like what?" she asked.

"Like anything."

So she brought over the ketchup bottle. I told her it was a good choice, because even a bottle of ketchup is made up of parts. (In truth, anything she had chosen would have been a great choice, because everything in the universe can be broken into part–whole.) I asked her to name all the parts she could isolate. She came up with a good list: a plastic bottle, a cap, two sticker labels, the red stuff (the ketchup itself), and all the ingredients that make up the stuff. She was splitting the whole into parts.

I then guided her to isolate any one of those parts to notice that it, too, was made up of parts. She chose the cap. We noted that it was made of plastic, a top and a bottom, a hinge, a hole that lets the ketchup through, a little bump that fits into the hole to seal it shut, and those spirals at the cap's base that let you screw the cap onto the bottle top. "Cool," said Gianna. She had taken a single part, transformed it into a whole, and broken it further into smaller parts. From there, we looked at the problems with fractions to see how she could transfer her understanding of part-whole to her homework. She learned that any number or thing could be broken into parts; for example, 10 could be broken into ten 1s. But also, that 10 could be broken down in a different way such as five 2s. Depending on how she rendered the parts, the fractions could be different; using Cheerios, or M&Ms, or even little squares, she could see that 2/5 and 4/10 were numerically the same.

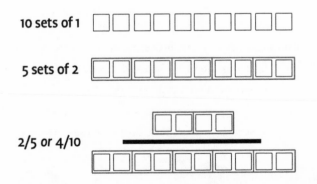

That night, Gianna sat up in bed when her mom was tucking her in. Laura momentarily suspected her daughter was stalling to stave off the inevitable bed time, but in fact Gianna was inspired. She couldn't stop herself from applying her new understanding of part-whole relationships to her bedroom. "Look, Mom, my room is made of walls, and a ceiling, a rug, a bed, a door . . . And if you just take the door as a whole, it's made up of its own parts: wood, paint, a doorknob, hinges . . . And you can take one of those parts as a whole, too, like the doorknob, and it's made of metal, the knob, little screws. . . . You could just keep doing this for everything in the room." Gianna had gotten it completely. We find that she's typical: children love part-whole thinking and have a lot of fun with it.

The Physical Universe Is Nested In Part-Whole

> *If only one idea had to be passed on to the next generation, it is the concept of Atoms and Molecules, and that everything is made of them.*
>
> —Richard Feynman

Gianna relayed the part-whole structure of her room by looking at it in both directions. We can and should do this with any object or idea. We can look "up" and see the whole that something is a part of, and up again to see a whole that contains that whole as one of its parts. Or we can look "down" and see the parts that

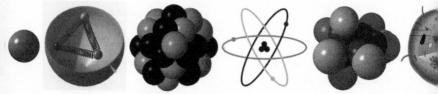

make up that something. And look down again, and again, to see the parts of the parts.

Early Indian and Greek philosophers thought the universe was made up of indivisible atoms. The word atom literally means "not-cuttable": *a* meaning "not" and *tomos* meaning "to cut." In the seventeenth and eighteenth centuries, chemists offered a physical theory of the atom's indivisibility. But in the nineteenth and twentieth centuries, physicists discovered that the atom has structure and subatomic components. Knowledge changes: the atom is cuttable after all.

On the other end of the spectrum, the word universe, literally meaning "one whole," was originally chosen to denote "everything." The universe was the whole of wholes. Anything you could think of was part of the universe. The universe was the final whole; the only whole that didn't serve as a part of anything larger. Wrong again. Knowledge changes. Today, cosmologists, physicists, astronomers, philosophers, theologians, and fiction writers propose a multiverse (or meta-universe) that includes multiple universes. It seems our whole universe is merely a partial speck of dust in a much larger metaverse of metaverses. From the subatomic to the super-universal, part-whole structure prevails. From the infinitesimal to the infinite, parts are nested in wholes and those wholes are in turn nested in larger wholes.

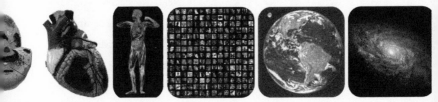

A classic toy that exemplifies the nested nature of systems is the matryoshka doll, or the Russian nested doll. "Matryoshka" is a nickname derived from "Matryona," a name in Russian culture that evokes a stout and sturdy woman. These beautiful dolls are cylindrical in shape (tapering just a bit at the neck) and open via a horizontal slit in the middle. Faces, arms, hair or head wraps, and dresses are painted on.

The largest doll contains all the others. The child opens her to reveal the next, opens that one to reveal the next, and so on until the "baby" is reached. Each inner doll is a whole containing others. Each doll is also a part of the whole matryoshka unit.

As an educational toy, matryoshka dolls are ingenious, containing within them not only multiple dolls but the potential for true transformative learning. Simply put, it changes children's minds. With a little facilitation, kids handling these dolls will come to know one of the most essential of all principles: the universe itself has a part-whole structure. Matryoshka dolls, and other tools that allow students to physically manipulate part-whole, transform children into *splumpers* (see page 66).

The Knowledge of the Universe Is Nested in Part-Whole

Although scientists do use deep, analytical methods to determine knowledge structures, such sophistication is hardly required to see what is right before our eyes. For example, if we simply scour an encyclopedia and remove all of its images and line them up in a grid, we can see that despite the diversity of topics and disciplines, each image clearly indicates part-whole structure.

We don't need special technology or tools to see this universal structure.

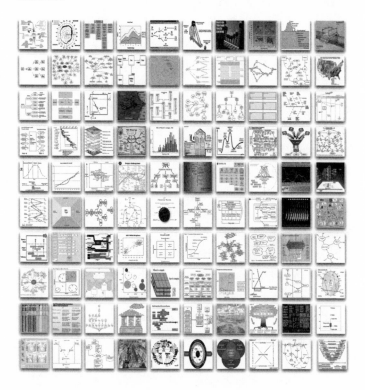

The knowledge we construct is a representation of our real physical universe. It's not perfect—we are always learning more about things and changing what we know—but it is approximate. In other words, although our knowledge is imperfect, there is correspondence between what we know and what is real. It makes sense then that the universal patterns we find in the structure of knowledge would parallel structures in the universe.[24]

Splitters and Lumpers Make Splumpers

There's an old saying in science that although there are many types of scientists, there are fundamentally only two kinds of scientists: *splitters* and *lumpers*. Splitters are those scientists who reduce the whole into parts, splitting it up into manageable bites for analysis and study. Lumpers are the integrators. They find parts and lump them together. In the 21st century, we need our students and scientists to be *splumpers*. Gianna is a splumper. Richard Feynman was a splumper. You and your students can be splumpers, too. You need only to think in systems of part and whole.

The phrase organizing systems doesn't conjure up anything terribly meaningful or robust in and of itself. But, understanding the simple elements of systems—part and whole—is a universal pattern of thinking; all fields of knowledge are systems made up of parts and wholes, whether they are physical and structural or abstract and conceptual. All knowledge has part-whole structure, and therefore to understand it, we must see the part-whole structure of each and every idea we encounter. It is easy to see if we look for it, because at every level of scale the universe is organized into a part-whole structure.

We all organize things into systems. We can't help it. The universe provides many opportunities to do so, given that it all contains part-whole structure. All fields of knowledge use systems to self-organize. Thus, as students need to understand knowledge, they must be able to split ideas into component parts AND lump parts in to new ideas. This act of "splumping" leads to a far deeper understanding of all knowledge and creates thinkers who can solve complex problems with robust solutions.

FIVE

The Patterns of Thinking Method
Taking Perspectives

The other day a snail got mugged by two turtles (yes, turtle crime is on the rise). The police rushed to the scene of the crime and asked the bewildered snail what had happened.

"I don't know," said the snail. "It all happened so fast."

How long did it take you to laugh? A few seconds? Your brain is remarkable. In order to get this joke, you had to take three perspectives in an instant. First, you understood the idea of speed from the perspective of a snail, then speed from the perspective of a turtle, and finally, your own perspective on speed as a human being. Your brain took three perspectives within a second. It is an efficient, perspective-taking machine. It even does it without us knowing that we needed to do it in the first place! Your mind sorted through three perspectives and put them together in a flash, causing you to laugh.

Jokes aside, perspective taking—the fourth pattern of thinking—is universal to all thoughts and exists in the knowledge we interact with every day. It also has great importance in our society; it lies at the root of all prosocial behavior such as empathy and compassion. Societies would not survive without perspective. Beyond that, bias, mindset, stereotypes, paradigms, mediation, negotiation, lock-in, scale, context, and worldview are all based on perspective. It follows then that an ability to make perspectives explicit increases creativity, innovation, conflict resolution skills, and prosocial behavior for children and adults.

Like all the patterns of thinking, perspectives can be hidden. Sometimes we simply lose track of them, forgetting we used them to arrive at a particular conclusion in the first place (like the snail joke). When this happens, we risk getting into a sort of bias cul-de-sac which hinders our ability to "see" what's really going on. Like distinctions, relationships, and systems, perspectives are simple and sublime.

Take a Point *and* a View

We often think that we have a point of view. We do. But we often miss a critical point of understanding about perspective. A perspective is comprised of a point *and* a view. The point is the subject, or the position from which the idea is viewed; the view is the object, or what is viewed. Because the point affects the view and vice versa, we expand what we know about any idea in profound ways when we become conscious of both point and view. A point of view is not a static thing; it is actually the relationship between two structural elements: Perspectives = point + view.

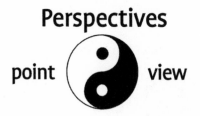

Perspectives

point   view

Taking perspective is viewing the world or anything in it from a particular point of view. There are physical perspectives, anthropomorphic, and conceptual perspectives. While we are used to thinking of different people as having differing perspectives, note that every idea has its own perspective as well. Anything we think about, we look at through the perspective or lens of another idea, or a conceptual perspective. In other words, we always look at one idea through another idea. Consider the "Civil War" or the "War between the States," names that reflect the Northern perspective and carry the connotations of a nation divided, torn apart, brother versus brother. Consider the Southern perspective on the very same war. They call it the "war of Northern aggression," which has a different connotation, where the Northern states are seen as instigators of the war. Teaching our students to see an idea from many perspectives shows them that how we name things, and the parts we see of an idea are a result of the perspective from which we view it.

When you have a point and a view, you have a perspective. There is no considering or thinking about anything without standing at a point from where we view it. As with any relationship, the point affects the view and the view in turn affects the point; they impact and change each other.

A Change in Perspective Changes Everything

We can look at the same thing (or concept) from different perspectives to magnify its various aspects. Then we come to understand it better. The painting *The Starry Night*, by Vincent Van Gogh, is shown here from various perspectives. We can look at the painting in terms of shape; in terms of line; and in terms of color.

Taking different perspectives is something teachers can do with students from preK to PhD. An innovative elementary teacher added another perspective; feelings. So students zeroed in on elements of the painting and the feelings it evoked in each of them. The nine frames at the bottom are from a doctoral dissertation that analyzes the colors of *The Starry Night*.

Categories Are a Perspective

Categorization is not universal like the patterns of thinking, but it is very popular. We organize our desktop in categories by putting files in folders. We categorize the items found in a supermarket into similar areas (produce, meats, toiletries, etc.). We spend a great deal of time teaching students to sort and categorize. Yet, we seldom make it explicit that a perspective is necessary whenever we categorize something.

Students engaged in categorizing or sorting tasks are practicing what one type of grown-up scientists give their life's work to: categorizing life forms. The general public relies on the following system: Kingdom, Phylum, Class, Order, Family, Genus, and Species. Yet scientists called systematists have 21 competing and valid ways to categorize organisms into species. Each of these 21 ways to categorize is based on a perspective, such as morphology (appearance). There are numerous exceptions to the rule and many types of organisms that just don't fit these schemes. For example, nearly all fungi and bacteria are generally indifferent to species boundaries. Indeed, there are so many implicit perspectives in species categorization that systematist Allen MacNeill makes the radical proposition that "individual living organisms are the only things that exist in the natural world, and that species (including animal species) are quite literally figments of the human imagination."

The point is this. When toddlers categorize picture cards or children categorize toys, or adolescents categorize baseball cards, or adults categorize computer files, or scientists categorize findings, all are using the same skill: taking perspective.

The World According to Whom?

According to Vladimiro Valerio, a cartography expert from the University of Venice, there's no such thing as a map without perspective: "Cartographers don't lie," he said, "but they take a position."[25] This quote appeared in a New York Times article featuring a globe-making outfit, "one of the biggest and best-known companies in the business," called Nova Rico. It's based in a small Italian town near the city of Florence. Nova Rico's globes land in classrooms all over the world, the United States included.

The company's directors reveal some of the fascinating distinctions they're required to make based on perspective: For Palestinians and some other Arabian countries, it's commonplace to omit Israel altogether—an egregious omission, its very existence going unrecognized. Cyprus is divided in two for Turkish customers; but if Greeks commission the globe, it stays whole. Certain parts of Antarctica may be assigned to either Chile or Argentina— depends on who's buying. Once, the company was threatened with a boycott from Iran because a globe called the gulf between that country and Saudi Arabia the "Arabian Gulf" instead of the "Persian Gulf."[26]

Adopting a particular perspective can have weighty consequences. The perspectives we take, the perspectives we recognize or ignore, and those that we allow others to make for us, lie at the root of our biases and stereotypes, our worldview and mindset. Like all the patterns of thinking, seeing both elements of perspective, point and view, deepens understanding in any area of study and creates students who will challenge lines that are drawn for them, check their own assumptions, and be more thoughtful as a whole.

 **SIX**

Thinking at Every Desk

Ripple Effect

In our professional development trainings around the country and the world, we are often asked by teachers, "Why does this method work so well in my classroom?" The reason they ask is that the results they see in the classroom seem to go well beyond simply teaching thinking skills. Teachers see increased student engagement. They see their students going beyond memorizing facts to deep understanding of topical content. They see test scores increase. They see their own effectiveness and engagement as teachers increase. Many have told us that the Patterns of Thinking Method has re-ignited that intangible love of learning and teaching that initially drew them to be teachers. They want to know why these impacts are occurring just from using a method. We explain it this way. When teachers use the Patterns of Thinking Method, their energy is focused on the two most effective relationships in education today.

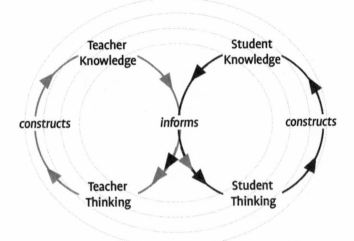

They are: 1) the student-teacher relationship, and 2) the knowledge-thinking relationship.

When we focus on these two relationships, the ripple effect is that we get many best practices for free without explicitly trying to get them. Just a few of these best practices include:

- differentiated instruction,
- student-centered learning,
- multiple intelligences,
- teacher effectiveness,
- data-driven assessment,
- deep understanding
- 21st-century skills,
  - critical thinking,
  - creative thinking,

- interdisciplinary thinking,
  - systems thinking,
  - scientific thinking,
  - prosocial thinking,
- learning by design, and
- improved test scores.

All of these effects are a natural output of zeroing in on these two relationships.

We've already discussed the knowledge-thinking relationship. It is an inseparable and dynamic cycle. When we think, we build more knowledge. We become more knowledgeable. At the same time, this knowledge helps us to think even better. It's a positively reinforcing loop with exponential payoffs. Equally important is that by focusing on the thinking and knowledge creation of the child, we are building the relationship between teacher and student. It is this relationship that acts as the central conduit for learning. But why would this lead to such remarkable benefits and best practices?

René Descartes, the father of modern Western science said, "I think, therefore I am." Buddha, the father of Eastern philosophy said, "We are what we think. With our thoughts we create the world." What both of them reveal is the absolutely essential role thinking plays in shaping our identity. This holds true for our students. A teacher who is keyed-in to what and how their student is thinking, is seeing their students for who they are. As a result, students feel recognized when their thoughts are acknowledged and valued by their teacher. This increases not only competence in any subject matter, but also the student's confidence when approaching new knowledge. When students are encouraged to think about their own thinking, they are learning about themselves.

If the relationship between teacher and student is focused on knowledge and thinking then the focal point of learning is on the students' construction in relation to the goal of the knowledge being learned (a fact, the Civil War, Pythagorean Theorem, seasonal change, whatever). If the teacher and student have a method to recognize and communicate the construction of an idea then they can do three things of great importance. First, they can see the [intended] construction of the idea that is the goal of learning (say, seasonal change). Second, they can see the student's construction of the idea. And third, they can compare and contrast the two in order to assess where thinking must be directed or corrected. For example, research at Harvard University found that in order to understand seasonal change, students must identify 11 ideas and relate them in a systematic way.[27] This research found that 21 of the 23 graduates, alumni, and faculty interviewed could not properly identify, relate, and systematize these 11 concepts to answer the question, "why do we have seasons?" Their knowledge of seasonal change was different from the valid knowledge of seasonal change—it was mismatched. Identifying the mismatch between the goal ideas (the test, etc.) and the students' construction of the ideas is universally important in education and holds true for any topic or idea in any grade from preK to PhD. We can call this type of comparison, "construct matching"—where we map the student's thinking onto the factual knowledge that will be on the test.

Education today is complex, and it's easy to get caught up in the hub-bub of the administrivia, the newest technological gizmo, the debates on classroom size or this or that theory, budgets, and behavioral problems. The Patterns of Thinking Method cuts through all the noise and helps us to find the signal. When we use the Patterns of Thinking Method in the classroom, the focus of education is where it should be—on the students' constructions of the world and on teacher effectiveness in helping children to build knowledge.

Becoming a Ninja

The Patterns of Thinking Method is simple but it is also sublime. It has deep implications that will not only change your teaching but also your life. We call the process of gaining mastery in the Patterns of Thinking Method, "becoming a Ninja" because the process requires the same discipline, dedication, and practice as becoming a clandestine assassin. The first step in becoming a Ninja, we call "white belt." As a white belt, you should understand each pattern of thought (distinction, system, relationship, perspective or DSRP) and its two elements (identity-other, cause-effect, part-whole, point-view). You should be aware of the aspects of each pattern that tend to be ignored, forgotten, or overlooked. For example, we often see identity, but miss the other. We often recognize the parts of something but fail to see the whole. Relationships are notoriously invisible. And, as much as we hate to admit it, we humans often lack the ability to get or take perspective. You should understand that the basic "equation" is the same for each pattern of thought: Pattern = element + element. The interaction between elements and their relationship to the pattern is best characterized by the Tao—yin and yang—where each element not only interacts with each other but also contains the other. That is, when we look at the yin and yang "swooshes" we see that yin contains a little bit of yang and yang contains a little bit of yin, and both are mutually dependent on each other.

Think about it. For every identity there is an other ... but that other can have its own identity. The same underlying structure is evident in the remaining patterns and elements. Every cause can also be seen as an effect; every part a whole, and vice versa; and, in simple terms, everything we look at (conceptually at least) is capable of looking back at us. Finally, white belts must understand two important ideas. First, that the Patterns of Thinking are agnostic to age, grade, subject area, or style and type of learner. When they understand this, they begin to see the vertical articulation of these thinking skills from the preK level to PhD. Second, they should understand the importance of knowledge and why seeing the constructions of students is synonymous with seeing the student. Seeing the student means the student will be engaged and motivated to learn. That, in a nutshell, is the remarkable role of the teacher; to engage the student in lifelong learning. Once white belts understand these two ideas, they will see that it's worth putting in the effort required to ascend to black belt.

The second step in becoming a Patterns of Thinking Ninja is becoming a "yellow belt". The key to becoming a yellow belt is to integrate and apply the patterns. Each pattern alone is powerful, but the real impact of the Patterns of Thinking Method comes from *integrating* the four patterns. The yellow belt Ninja understands how dynamic DSRP is. Not only can each element of each Pattern take on the role of the other, but every element and Pattern can take on the role of any other element and Pattern. For example, both an identity and an other can be a system, made up of parts. An identity can also be a relationship, in the same way that I might be the relationship between two friends that do not know each other. An identity can of course have its own unique perspective, too.

The yellow belts also understand the *application* of DSRP to content and the impact it can have across grade levels (vertical articulation) and subject areas (transfer). When we apply DSRP to content knowledge we begin to see "common structures"—the same conceptual structures that underlie very different content. That is, we might see the same structural, conceptual patterns in mathmatics that we see in language arts, social science, or the physical sciences. We might see the same conceptual pattern in a conflict at work that exists in a conflict at home. The value of this is exponential—consider that finding a solution to the work conflict will also be a solution to the home conflict, thereby "killing two birds with one stone." Students might learn, for example, a common structure for a political argument (such as a proposition, evidence, and authority), that is exclusive of the specific content, and therefore can be used for the rest of their lives, even when the specific argument is long since forgotten.

Red-belt Ninjas are well on their way toward mastery. All the knowledge and skills of the white and yellow belt Ninjas is deepened and refined. The red belt may plan for lessons using Patterns of Thinking and may purposefully incorporate the thinking into every lesson but what really makes the red belts decidedly different is their ability to recognize and do DSRP spontaneously and to assess it.

Black-belt Ninjas are masters. The progression of belts follows a well-known learning curve based on competence and consciousness. The learning curve consists of four stages. First, the learners are *unconsciously incompetent*; they do not know what they do not know, and as a result they do not have competence in the topic or skill. Second, is the *consciously incompetent* stage, in which the learner has suddenly awoken to new knowledge but has not yet garnered the skills to apply it. In the third stage, *conscious competence*, the learner is not only conscious but has also gained the knowledge, attitude, and skills necessary to apply it. The black belt Ninjas know, integrate, and apply the Patterns of Thinking Method in any domain without conscious effort. Their competence is an extension of themselves. As the venerable Yoda explained, "Do or do not. There is no try." The black belt Ninja need not try because he is. He is a sage in the *unconsciously competent* stage.

Practice, Practice, Practice

What does each stage of Ninjahood share in common? Practice, practice, practice. We've covered the elemental structure and importance of each of the four patterns of thinking. Now it's time to translate your understanding of these ideas into skills you can use in the classroom. It's one thing to gain the knowledge of the Patterns of Thinking. But, to develop the skills that will transform your teaching and your students, you need to practice. We wish we had a quick fix for you in how to do it. But like most skills, the trick to "getting it" isn't a trick at all—getting it requires practice. The teachers we see who have the most success with the Patterns of Thinking Method are those that dive in and start practicing it without fear of making mistakes. That's true for gaining mastery in any topic. There are lots of resources you can use to get started and we are always making these resources better. Here are five things you can do to develop and deepen your practical use of the Patterns of Thinking Method.[28]

1. Let 8 Easy Questions Guide You

We find that even the best of teachers are often *one question away* from guiding a student to a deeper understanding of topical content. Guiding questions frame the student-teacher dialogue to elicit and explicate a student's thinking processes. In the short run, this allows teachers to diagnose and correct a student's construction of relevant content, and ultimately to assess thinking skills in their classroom. The advantage to students is far more important and far reaching. They learn not only how to think, but also how to think *about* their thinking. Each pattern of thinking has two guiding questions. Once you've learned all eight, you can begin mixing and matching to create an infinite number of possibilities —we like to say, "*From 8 to ∞.*"

GUIDING QUESTIONS FOR			
Distinctions	**Systems**	**Relationships**	**Perspectives**
What is _____ ?	Does _____ have parts?	Is _____ related to _____ ?	From the perspective of _____ , [insert question]?
What is not _____ ?	Can you think of _____ as a part?	Can you think of _____ as a relationship?	Can you think about _____ from a different perspective?

EXAMPLES OF QUESTIONS COMBINING D, S, R, AND P	
Distinctions + **R**elationships	In what ways is _____ different from _____?
	In what ways is _____ *not* different from _____?
	In what ways is _____ similar to _____?
	In what ways is _____ *not* similar to _____?
	What is the relationship between _____ and _____?
	What is *not* the relationship between _____ and _____?
Distinctions + **S**ystems	What are some of the parts that _____ is made up of?
	What are *not* some of the parts that _____ is made up of?
	What is _____ a part of?
	What is _____ *not* a part of?
	What are some [parts, examples, attributes, descriptors] of _____?
	What are *not* some [parts, examples, attributes, descriptors] of _____?
Distinctions + **S**ystems + **P**erspectives	From a different perspective, what are the parts of _____?
Distinctions + **S**ystems + **R**elationships	What are some parts of the relationship between _____ and _____?
	What are *not* some parts of the relationship between _____ and _____?
Distinctions + **S**ystems + **R**elationships + **P**erspective	From a different perspective, what are some parts of the relationship between _____ and _____?

2. Take small bites

The standards and skills of each pattern of thought allow you to focus in on discrete skills in smaller bites. Standards and skills are skills that each student (and teacher) should be able to do. You can use skills to break each Pattern of Thinking down into bite-sized components. Each of these standards and skills is vertically articulated—that means that the skill itself is as important to preschoolers as it is to PhDs. Sure, the content knowledge will become increasingly more sophisticated, but the underlying pattern of thought remains the same.

Of equal importance is that each of these skills is also easily assessable and can be used in formative assessments, informal and spontaneous evaluations, and more formal progress reports and tests. For a complete list of the standards and skills see the section on National Standards for Thinking.

3. Read More Vignettes

We presented a few vignettes for each pattern of thought in this book, but there are hundreds more and we're always finding new great examples. Vignettes are a great way to see the many diverse places where we might find "D, S, R, and P."

4. See It to Believe It

Sometimes teachers just need to see other teachers do it in order to "get it." Watch video case studies of teachers in the classroom using Patterns of Thinking and ThinkBlocks. You can see examples of actual teachers doing actual lessons with actual students in any number of topics and grades from Head Start to Advanced Placement.

5. Become a Ninja

Get trained in the Patterns of Thinking Method. We offer white, yellow, red, and black belt trainings for teachers. One training will transform your teaching. A few will transform your life.

Expect results

Knowing the results you can expect is helpful in looking for them. Infusion of the Patterns of Thinking Method throughout a standards based curriculum will have the following impact in your classroom or school:

1. Students are more engaged.
2. They understand the content more deeply.
3. Their knowledge retention increases.
4. Their transfer of learning increases.
5. They develop skills in metacognition, understanding how they think.
6. Teachers can reach any type of learner.
7. Teacher preparation is simplified.
8. A vertical articulation of essential thinking skills occurs across the grades in all subject areas.
9. Thinking skills become easy to measure with a practical way to assess how students are constructing meaning.

The Patterns of Thinking Method develops essential skills for your students' success in the 21st century. It simplifies teaching for teachers and learning for students. Everyone benefits.

National Standards for Thinking Skills

Now that we have a method, we also have a discrete set of things to measure. Because the Patterns of Thinking and guiding questions offer an algorithm for sophisticated thinking, they also provide a discrete set of standards and skills that can be measured.

STANDARD	SKILL
Learns to make *distinctions* by identifying what is and is not included in an idea.	Names and defines concepts by communicating what something is and is not.
	Considers alternative boundaries between what is and is not part of an idea.
	Understands that every thing is a distinction comprised of identity and other.
Learns to think about inter-*relationships* between and among ideas.	Relates ideas.
	Identifies and names hidden relationships between and among ideas.
	Identifies the parts of a relationship.
	Understands that every idea can be related to other ideas or act as a relationship.
Learns to think in *systems* by organizing parts and wholes.	Identifies the parts of ideas.
	Organizes systems into parts and wholes.
	Recognizes the alternative wholes that a part can belong.
	Understands that every whole has parts and every part is a whole.

Standard	Skill
Learns to take different points-of-view and see new *perspectives*	Takes multiple perspectives on a topic or issue.
	Understands that perspective is comprised of both a point and a view.
	Demonstrates taking various types of perspectives (physical, psycho-social, conceptual)
	Recognizes that a perspective exists even when it is unstated.
Integrates the Patterns of Thinking	Demonstrates ability to combine distinction making, interrelating, part-whole organization, and perspective taking processes to create, understand, and change concepts
Applies the Patterns of Thinking to Content Knowledge	Is aware of both content and structural context when constructing the meaning of any idea.

The standards and skills are universally important from PreK to PhD, for every student. Any age. Any grade. Any subject area. Any type of learner. The Patterns of Thinking give us the ability to establish National Standards for Thinking Skills.

From Either-Or to And-Both Thinking

"The test of a first-rate intelligence is the ability to hold two opposed ideas in the mind at the same time, and still retain the ability to function."

—F. Scott Fitzgerald

Research conducted with college students from both Kyoto, Japan and Michigan demonstrates the significant differences between Eastern and Western styles of thought. Students were shown videos depicting an underwater scene that contained fast and slow fish, water, bubbles, plant life, rocks, and so on. Japanese and American students described the scene differently. While both mentioned the fish (the "identity") equally, Japanese students also mentioned background components (the "other") 60 percent more often than the Americans. Japanese students also mentioned the hidden relationships with surrounding objects ("the fish wove through the grasses") twice as often. The study also noted that Japanese students spoke first of the environment ("it's a scene in a pond"), while American students first mentioned the fish.

The study concluded that, "Asians see the big picture and they see objects in relation to their environments—so much so that it can be difficult for them to visually separate objects from their environments. Westerners focus on objects while slighting the field and they literally see fewer objects and relationships in the environment than do Asians." [29]

It's tempting to conclude that one thought style is better than the other but the truth is that the 21st century calls for both types of thinking: thinking that helps us to see both the identity and the other, to see the hidden connections, to zoom in and to zoom out, to split and to lump, to take various perspectives. In short, the 21st-century thinker needs to hold two opposed ideas in the mind at the same time, and still retain the ability to function.

Our legal system (guilty, not guilty), technology, (1s and 0s), and worldview (us, them) to name a few, are all based on bivalency—the either-or logic of Aristotle (true, false). When we consider the 21st-century thinking skills we need in order to navigate effectively within our increasingly interconnected planet, it behooves us to expand our vision in both the macro and the micro. It's the power of multivalency or and-both. The power of the Patterns of Thinking Method is the power of and-both. The four patterns allow us to create definitive boundaries in one moment and challenge those boundaries in the next. In the end, we hold both in full view. The implications of this multivalent or "and-both" thinking cannot be underestimated—with "and-both" we can create mental models that are more accurate to the real world. In short, mental models that are out of alignment with the real world are useless. Mental models that are aligned with the real world can be used to navigate and change it.

Implant or Inoculation?

The Patterns of Thinking are universal to all thought. They are as powerful as they are ubiquitous. I often like to say that they are "hidden in plain sight." The power of these patterns lies in seeing them all around us. We must shift our thinking to see not just the identity of something but the implied—and often purpose-fully-ignored—other. Of equal importance is our ability to see the multitude of potential relationships between ideas and to recognize relationships that are implied by others on our behalf. When organizing systems we must see the parts in the wholes and the whole in the parts. Finally, and of no less importance, is our understanding that a perspective is comprised of a point *and* a view. If we fail to teach our students these four patterns universal to all thinking, we allow others to use the patterns against them.

implant

noun |'im,plant|
ORIGIN late Middle English : from late Latin implantare 'engraft,' from Latin in- 'into' + plantare 'to plant.'
To establish or fix (an idea) in a person's mind.

In other words, these very patterns can be used as implants to manipulate our youth, and ourselves, for attention, money, or votes.

Just as the four patterns of thinking can be used with deleterious effect, they also serve as an inoculation against the rampant manipulation that permeates our media and society today.

inoculation

noun |inoculation|
ORIGIN late Middle English: from Latin inoculat- 'engrafted,' from the verb inoculare, from in- 'into' + oculus 'eye, bud.'
The act or an instance of inoculating, especially the introduction of an antigenic substance or vaccine into the body to produce immunity to a specific disease.

We can inoculate our students to offset the risk of cognitive implants by teaching them four simple rules that are the patterns of their thinking. We must teach students to:

- Take another look at the other,
- Discover hidden connections between ideas,
- See both the parts and wholes that make up a system, and
- Take many perspectives on any and every idea they encounter.

It is therefore essential for educators working with the patterns of thinking to bring to light the hidden identities and others of our *distinctions*, the hidden parts and wholes of our *systems*, the hidden cause-and-effect *relationships* we draw, and the hidden points and views that make up our *perspectives*. These hidden patterns—left unrecognized—pose the single biggest threat we have faced to this day. We run the danger of continuing to be an un-thinking society. In America, that is unacceptable.

Think. It's Patriotic.

I am not pulling your leg. I'm writing these words for this paragraph (and a few of the others) on July 4th. I'm sitting in my backyard. I need to take a shower and get ready for a big barbecue. Earlier, as I do each year, I read the Declaration of Independence. A refresher. It's a remarkable document. One can imagine the Founding Fathers knew they were in for a fight when writing it. They were thinkers, not warmongers. But they were fed up.

In the Declaration of Independence, when the term united States of America is used, the writers did not capitalize the word "united" as we do today. It was an adjective that described the States of America, rather than part of the proper noun it is today. But what really unites us as Americans—what makes me feel a sense of patriotism—are the ideas expounded upon in a small paragraph in the Declaration:

> *We hold these truths to be self-evident, that all men are cre-*
> *ated equal, that they are endowed by their Creator with certain*
> *unalienable Rights, that among these are Life, Liberty and the*

pursuit of Happiness. —That to secure these rights, Govern-
ments are instituted among Men, deriving their just powers from
the consent of the governed . . .

Deriving their just powers from the consent of the governed. That's a powerful concept and it is as American as it gets. But here's the point, and I get chills as I write it: if the governed are not thinking, then their consent is meaningless. Thinking is as patriotic and American as apple pie.

Thinking at Every Desk

Ole Kirk Christiansen, a carpenter, founded Lego in 1932. At the time, he was out of work because of the Depression and decided to build wooden toys (piggy banks, etc.) in Denmark. In 1947 Ole got samples of a plastic brick invented and patented ("self locking building bricks") by Mr. Hilary "Harry" Fisher Page in Britain, and began creating the automatic binding bricks which we know today as Lego Bricks, a name that originated in 1953. Today Lego, with headquarters is Billund, Denmark, is the sixth largest toy company in the world, with over 5,000 employees and revenue of $7.8 billion Danish Kroner.

When we were kids Lego Building Bricks came in a big bucket. You could build anything! In fact, Ole's 1958 Lego patent 3005282 states, "the principle object of the invention is to provide for a vast variety of combinations of the bricks for making toy structures of many different kinds and shapes." And that was the magic of Lego. Anything you could imagine, you could build. Every kid could unleash his creativity on the world. Children today may never know the joy of unbridled creativity. Licensing has become one of the toy industry's most lucrative venues, and Lego is no exception. Inundated with over 130 new licensed Lego kits per year, children can choose among Thomas and Friends, Bob the Builder, Batman, Star Wars, Indiana Jones, and SpongeBob SquarePants, only to be guided by step-by-step instructions, using the same amount of creativity needed to read a VCR manual. In contrast to the unbounded play mentioned in the original patent, these licensed kits only allow children to build pre-designed structures.

This is not to say that Lego's new licensed products lack creativity. Indeed the designer's desk at Lego's headquarters are teeming with creative ideas. Perhaps for profit or consumer demand Lego has changed its business strategy, but the net effect for children around the world is that what was once open to imagination is now closed by instruction. The physical construction is now scripted, robbing children of the cognitive construction that was once the point. The result is that the creativity and construction that once filled the hands and minds of children everywhere, now rests at a corporate desk in Denmark.

Here's our fear. That educators, teachers, curriculum designers and others—all with the best of intentions—are doing an analogous thing in preparing content for classroom consumption. We're surgically removing the messy constructions. Thinking happens, but it happens at the wrong desk. It needs to happen at the student's desk. The Lego story serves as poignant reminder to curriculum designers and teachers everywhere: when we over-prepare for the class, we are robbing our students of the opportunity to build their own ideas. We must insure that the construction happens at the right desk, not the teacher's or curriculum designer's desk. Without thinking at every student's desk, your graduates will not be invited to sit at those tables of the future.

21st-century Teams at Tables

We live in a fast-paced, globalized world where knowledge is growing and changing at a rate we can't keep up with. Our schools need to prepare students for jobs that don't exist, that will use technology not yet invented, to solve unknown problems in a society we can only imagine. In this 21st century, students need not only to know the content knowledge covered in school, they also will need to know how to think.

As research scientists, educators, entrepreneurs, and Americans, we've seen the need for thinking skills all around us—from preschool to middle school, from high school to college, from business leaders to world leaders. Today's students can ace any test but lack the ability to do the unstructured tasks that are so common in the real world. Thinking is not important just in schools but also for our businesses and our country as a whole. Thinking is patriotic—it lies at the core of our workforce and competitive advantage in the world.

In 2006, as colleagues at Cornell University, Laura Colosi and I decided to do something about the problems we face educationally and in the world at large. We decided to do something academics rarely do: to put our Ivory Tower research to work in the real-world. We started a small organization, called ThinkWorks, with a BIG vision: Thinking at every desk. Our vision is that every

American student learns to think. That's every student in every grade and every subject.

ThinkWorks is more than an organization, it's a catalyst to bring about audacious social change. We hope you will join us in our Vision to bring thinking skills to every student, school, and district in America. Start simple, by bringing thinking skills to the desks you have influence over. If you're a classroom teacher, that might be 20 or 30 students each year. If you are a principal or superintendent, you have the influence to bring thinking skills to many more desks. But if you are just one person, bring thinking skills into your own life. We only need one desk at a time to make a difference.

Building Blocks of Knowledge

One evening while Laura was making dinner, her six-year-old daughter (Gianna), who had been doing her homework, appeared next to her with ten little pieces of paper in her hand. The pieces were her spelling list: each scrap contained one word she was supposed to learn to spell. "Why did you do that to your spelling list?" Laura asked her. Gianna shrugged: "So I can do stuff with it." Gianna finds grasping abstract concepts, such as words, much easier if she can turn them into physical objects—in this case, into pieces of paper that she can hold, feel, and manipulate. Gianna is not alone. Although some students easily absorb abstract knowledge directly, many do not, and everybody can benefit from integrating the sense of touch into the learning process.

Research in education and cognitive science has shown that humans are "knowledge architects." We build knowledge through thinking and our interaction with information. As Gianna's story illustrates, the connection between tactile activity and conceptual construction is deeply instinctual. The modern field of haptics—the study of how humans use touch and kinesthetics to acquire information—has established that touch and movement are deeply connected with the process of constructing knowledge. Other findings reveal how movement, gesture, and vision play a role in the process of constructing knowledge. For example, a baby's exploration the world through touch begins as early as a few months of age and continues in various ways throughout childhood.[30]

Noted child psychologist, Jean Piaget, demonstrated that the use of the sense of touch through object manipulation increased children's ability to create mental constructs of the world (build knowledge) in different age groups.[31] One of Piaget's students, MIT professor Seymour Papert proposed not only that children build knowledge but that they need to construct it, literally, in physical forms or models. He emphasized that people learn most easily when they physically put things together, as with Lego or blocks. He concluded that better learning did not come from finding "better ways for the teacher to instruct, but from giving the learner better opportunities to construct."[32]

Laboratory and field studies have shown that integrating tactile activities into the classroom improves learning by bringing multiple sensory systems and areas of the brain into the learning process, improving retention and developing and reinforcing core thinking skills. Much research into haptic learning has established a connection among touch, kinesthetics, activity, and improved learning.[33] Learning through the haptic system is stronger than visual learning alone. This calls for attention to touch as an integral and important part of children's learning.

The connection between hand and mind already manifests in a myriad of tactile manipulatives seen in classrooms all over the world. Manipulative play in classrooms draws on haptics to make the crucial hand-mind connection, using the students' inherent multimodal tendency to relate movement to mental activity. Teachers have been using manipulatives—wooden blocks, math beads, sandpaper letters, coins—for as long as schools have existed, across many generations. Gianna created her own when she turned one long list of spelling words into moveable, touchable strips of paper. This act was purposeful, and she instinctively knew that she needed to do it to memorize, to be able to handle, that daunting list of words. Touch, as an integral part of thinking (and thus, learning) provides students with concrete experiences with intangible concepts and ideas.

Building Blocks of Knowledge

Using blocks or other common toys (such as Russian Matryoshka nesting dolls) can be powerful tools to develop thinking skills and encourage people to play with ideas. An analysis of 75 studies on the importance of block play shows that block play contributes to cognitive development and confirms that, "the benefits of [block] play has been well supported by the theories and research of the past century." This holds true today, as a recent American Academy of Pediatrics concludes, "Play is important to healthy brain development" and that through play, children use their creativity to develop "imagination, dexterity, and physical, cognitive, and emotional strength."

The construction paradigm reminds us that our hands are integrated with our brains. As such, doing, playing, and manipulating with the hands is an essential part of learning and thinking. Children actively build knowledge in a similar way to how they might construct a toy bridge out of toothpicks or to erect a crane out of various parts. In his autobiography, Frank Lloyd Wright speaks about the influence of toy building blocks in his early development. Generations of children learned about the built world, geometry, mathematics, architecture, design and creativity from such classics as Lincoln Logs, Lego Bricks, Tinker Toys, and Erector Sets. These construction sets introduced us to the built world. In the same way that children of the industrial age had toys to build physical structures, building knowledge requires a unique construction kit that allows children (and adults) to model, see, and manipulate ideas in their hands, which also develops important thinking skills.

A Construction Set for Ideas

When thoughts are inside our head, they risk being entangled with other thoughts, and it's hard to make sense of them and to think and communicate clearly. For centuries, teachers have used tactile manipulatives to represent ideas: marbles, Cheerios, flash cards, index cards, letter blocks, Post-it notes, or even sugar packets! ThinkBlocks are as easy to work with as any other items, but their physical design makes them a unique and powerful pedagogical tool. Their physical design manifests each of the four patterns of thinking. They can be used alone or with any existing realia or materials already in your classroom. They can be used as often as you like; or not, as we can just as easily teach with the Patterns of Thinking using only the guiding questions framework.

ThinkBlocks: A Revolutionary New Twist on Sugar Packets

ThinkBlocks are like sugar packets and other tactile manipulatives but with a revolutionary new twist. Unlike marbles, Cheerios, Post-it notes, index cards, and sugar packets, ThinkBlocks incorporate four universal Patterns of Thinking into their unique design. The result is an easy-to-use tactile manipulative that facilitates better thinking about any subject by any age learner. Here are five ways that ThinkBlocks are similar to and different from sugar packets:

1. Making Distinctions

Similarity: You can use both to represent any idea in a tactile way and distinguish that idea from other ideas.

Difference: Sugar packets are hard to write on, erase, and reuse.

2. Organizing Systems

Similarity: You can use both to model the parts of a whole.

Difference: It's hard to stuff one sugar packet inside of another, never mind two or more; whereas ThinkBlocks remind you about the part-whole structure of thinking.

3. Recognizing Relationships

Similarity: You can use both to think about relationships between and among ideas.

Difference: Because sugar packets are not magnetic like Think-Blocks are, they don't remind you to think about how one idea is connected to another.

4. Taking Perspectives

Similarity: You can use both to take different perspectives on any idea or thing.

Difference: Sugar packets don't have a reflective side that reminds you of the importance of perspective. ThinkBlocks do.

5. Patterns of Thinking Inside

Distinctions
identity & other

Systems
part & whole

Relationships
cause & effect

Perspectives
point & view

Similarity: Both are universal.

Difference: Whereas sugar packets are universal to restaurant tables everywhere, the unique design of ThinkBlocks is based on four Patterns of Thinking that are universal to how all people build, change, and understand ideas, mental models, and even mindsets and worldviews.

A Constructive Approach to Knowledge and Thinking

Taking a "constructive" approach to knowledge, where children are encouraged to build ideas, in a similar way that they might build a bridge or a skyscraper, will go a long way in developing the kinds of thinkers we need; thinkers who will thrive in the knowledge age. Experience and scientific research tells us that it is the ability to think and learn throughout life, not knowledge of this or that fact, that prepares us for solving life's challenges. Thinking is a skill that we all innately possess and rely on to manage our daily lives, master tasks, and navigate our way through the choices we make in life. Indeed, thinking is not only a matter of survival; it is essential to thriving in life.

ENDNOTES

1. This provocative quote is fascinating not only in content but because of its elusive source. It seems impossibly long not to properly sourced, and yet it has been used repeatedly in numerous publications and speeches without any attribution. As an approximation, we offer that it seems to have originated, though not verbatim, with former Secretary of Education Richard Riley.

2. Wolff, Edward N. "The Growth of Information Workers in the U.S. Economy, 1950–2000: the Role of Technological Change, Computerization, and Structural Change." *Communications of the ACM*, Volume 48, Issue 10, (October 2005) pp. 37–42

3. University of Vienna; dowload att http://news.bbc.co.uk/2/hi/uk_news/england/north_yorkshire/7498291.stm

4. Gough, D. (1991). Thinking about Thinking. Research Roundup, 7(2), 6.

5. Reproduced with permission, Sidney Harris, ScienceCartoonsPlus.com

6. Barnett, Thomas P.M., *The Pentagon's New Map: War and Peace in the Twenty-first Century*. (New York: G.P. Putnam's Sons, 2004).

7. http://www.thomaspmbarnett.com/pnm/map_index.htm (accessed September 30, 2008).

8. This number comes from a letter from the Chairman of the Coordinating Bureau of the Non-Aligned Movement, written in September of 2008. It can be seen at http://domino.un.org/unispal.nsf/47d4e277b48d9d3685256ddc00612265/38ecc57a3c2e3a7b852574da00718eff!OpenDocument (accessed January 9, 2009).

9. Komo 4 News and ABC News, "Missing Olympia Man Found in Denver," October 22, 2006, http://www.komonews.com/news/4454227.html (accessed November 7, 2008).

10. Suzanne Bloom, *A Bus for Us* (Honesdale, PA: Boyds Mills Press, 2001).

11. Many interesting examples exist of images that play with the concept of figure-ground or simply allow the viewer to play with perception by seeing things in different ways. Mooney faces, developed in the 1950s by cognitive psychologist Craig Mooney, have a certain strange beauty. These barely sketched-in black-and-white faces work on the principle of perceptual closure, a right-brain function by which we "fill in" missing information, sometimes with very little to rely on, to conceptualize a complete image. Studies have shown that when the faces are presented upside down or in other variant orientations, they become more difficult to grasp as whole images.

12. For Derek's detailed and entertaining presentation of the entire history of Pluto, go to http://www.thinkandthrive.com/tw/files/media/Pluto.pdf (accessed October 16, 2008).

13. The Adler Planetarium Statement About Pluto Reclassification. August 24, 2006: 26th General Assembly of the International Astronomical Union. p. 48. It was Michael Brown of MIT who made this discovery.

14. Chang, K (2006). Planet Discovered Last Year, Thought to Be Larger Than Pluto, Proves Roughly the Same Size. April 12, 2006. Downloaded at: http://www.nytimes.com/2006/04/12/science/space/12planet.html?_r=1 Chang also tells us that Xena had to be viewed through Hubble so that it could be identified. It was found to measure 2,400 km across, making it 5 percent larger than Pluto and 30 percent wider.

15. Adler, 2006, p. 49

16. To view Derek's online slide show online that guides you through this trek, go to http://www.thinkandthrive.com/kb/questions/15/What+are+Distinctions+%28D%29%3F (accessed October 16, 2008). On that page, find the section entitled "Walking a Fuzzy Distinction" and follow the link to the slide show.

17. Small interactions between different clumps of matter are called Van der Waals interactions. This is not Dutch for small but comes from the name of Dutch scientist Johannes Diderik van der Waals. To learn more about this phenomenon, go to http://en.wikipedia.org/wiki/Van_der_Waals_force (accessed November 7, 2008).

18. G. W. Cox and J. N. Katz, *Elbridge Gerry's Salamander: The Electoral Consequences of the Reapportionment Revolution* (Cambridge, U.K.: Cambridge University Press, 2002).

19. P. Harris. "Gerrymandering: How US politicians draw the electoral lines" [electronic version]. *Guardian Unlimited*, September 28. Retrieved February 9, 2007 from http://wf2dnvr4.webfeat.org/

20. See http://en.wikipedia.org/wiki/Bioinformatics (accessed January 24, 2009).

21. Bill Moggridge, *Designing Interactions* (Cambridge, MA: MIT Press, 2007). This quote comes from the front matter of the book, on the first page of text that precedes even roman numeral

pagination. It is not written by the author and no other author is named.

22. Ibid., 14.

23. Ibid.

24. And even that the structure of our brain that leads to these processes of thinking would adhere to the physical, chemical, biological, psychological, and sociological laws that either preceded it or evolved along side of its development.

25. Elisabetta Povoledo, "In Italy, Creating Worlds Takes Precision, Yes, and Politics," World sec., Europe, http://www.nytimes.com/2007/08/15/world/europe/15italy.html?ex=1344916800&en=6b2e3659850dbc10&ei=5124&partner=permalink&exprod=permalink (accessed October 27, 2008).

26. Ibid.

27. Schneps, M. (1989). Private universe project: Harvard University.

28. See http://www.ThinkingAtEveryDesk.com

29. Rochat, P. et al. (2003)The role of modelling and request type on symbolic comprehension of objects and gestures in young children. Journal of Child Language, 30, 27–45.

30. Ibid., 109.

31. Piaget, J. *The Construction of Reality in the Child.* (New York: Basic Books, 1954).

32. Papert, S. *The Connected Family.* (Atlanta: Longstreet Press, 1996).

33. Minogue, J. and Jones, M.G. 2006. "Haptics in Education: Exploring an Untapped Sensory Modality," *Review of Educational Research,* Vol. 76, No. 3, 317–348.